T0334150

Cambridge Elements ≡

Elements in Bioethics and Neuroethics
edited by
Thomasine Kushner
California Pacific Medical Center, San Francisco

ONE HEALTH ENVIRONMENTALISM

Benjamin Capps
Dalhousie University

CAMBRIDGE
UNIVERSITY PRESS

Shaftesbury Road, Cambridge CB2 8EA, United Kingdom

One Liberty Plaza, 20th Floor, New York, NY 10006, USA

477 Williamstown Road, Port Melbourne, VIC 3207, Australia

314–321, 3rd Floor, Plot 3, Splendor Forum, Jasola District Centre, New Delhi – 110025, India

103 Penang Road, #05–06/07, Visioncrest Commercial, Singapore 238467

Cambridge University Press is part of Cambridge University Press & Assessment, a department of the University of Cambridge.

We share the University's mission to contribute to society through the pursuit of education, learning and research at the highest international levels of excellence.

www.cambridge.org
Information on this title: www.cambridge.org/9781009547826

DOI: 10.1017/9781009271097

First published 2024

A catalogue record for this publication is available from the British Library.

ISBN 978-1-009-54782-6 Hardback
ISBN 978-1-009-27110-3 Paperback
ISSN 2752-3934 (online)
ISSN 2752-3926 (print)

One Health Environmentalism

Elements in Bioethics and Neuroethics

DOI: 10.1017/9781009271097
First published online: May 2024

Benjamin Capps
Dalhousie University

Author for correspondence: Benjamin Capps, benjamin.capps@dal.ca

Abstract: One Health emerges from the contingent scientific, social, and political realities of environmentalism. The concept mixes the land, sea, and sky with geopolitics on the global stages of the United Nations and World Health Organization. It inspires new investment in conservation and public health, motivates interdisciplinary collaboration, and in practice implicates green economies and animal law as well. This Element does not tackle all of this but attempts to situate One Health in the catastrophe of COVID-19; a socio-ecological upheaval prophetic of the inevitable next pandemic evolving from planetary climate crisis of our own making. *One Health Environmentalism* argues that humanity's future depends upon extending an olive branch to biotic communities, by being less speciesist and less blind to the rights in nature.

Keywords: One Health, environmentalism, public health, rights, nature

ISBNs: 9781009547826 (HB), 9781009271103 (PB), 9781009271097 (OC)
ISSNs: 2752-3934 (online), 2752-3926 (print)

Contents

1 Background: The Origin of One Health

Today, it seems possible to talk enthusiastically about One Health without a very clear idea of what it is.

It is September 2004. A group of health experts are meeting at a symposium at the Rockefeller University in New York City, to discuss 'Building Interdisciplinary Bridges to Health in a Globalized World'. A year before, the Severe Acute Respiratory Syndrome (SARS) outbreak was brought under control. The new coronavirus appeared suddenly in 2002, with the first human case of atypical pneumonia reported in Guangdong province in southern China. The outbreak might have started in civet cats (*Paguma larvata*), although the role of bats – *Chiroptera* – cannot be excluded. The international health community is now on high alert for new emergent infectious diseases, especially *zoonoses* that spread from animals to humans. The symposium is organized by the Wildlife Conservation Society (WCS) – first convened in 1895 as the New York Zoological Society – and its members are familiar with *hotspots* like geographical wilderness areas of high biodiversity, live animal or wet markets, and industrial farms, where infections – or *spillovers* – are most likely to occur. Their message is clear: zoonoses are normally viewed as public health matters, and although SARS suggests there are tools to stop a potential pandemic, the group is concerned about the increasing frequency of outbreaks and can prove that human activity is responsible. The increasing population scale of zoonotic infections, and spillovers of emergent infectious diseases, are not random, and are symptomatic of the Anthropocene, a geographical epoch recording human activity as the dominant influence on the planetary environment.[1] The idea of indomitable human impact, now accelerating beyond safe limits to all sustain life, is indicative of many years of human migration, exploration, industrialization, wars, and globalization.

Participants at the symposium wonder why ecological sciences have been ignored despite the growing evidence. They talk about sidelined studies, showcasing conservation as part of the solution. And many are alarmed about emerging cases of 'bird flu', the devastating outcomes if there were ever a large-scale Ebola Haemorrhagic Fever outbreak, or the emergence of a previously unknown disease.

At the Rockefeller University symposium, they agree that a different approach is needed, and they come up with *The Manhattan Principles*:

> [To] Recognize the essential link between human, domestic animal and wildlife health and the threat disease poses to people, their food supplies and economies, and the biodiversity essential to maintaining the healthy environments and functioning ecosystems we all require.[2]

They call it 'One Health–One World™'.

As a modern preoccupation, One Health plausibly sprung from One Medicine. According to this concept, 'veterinary medicine shares with public health a unique practice philosophy based upon identical population concepts'.[3] One Medicine influenced the epidemiology of veterinary public health in the 1940s,[4] and that field was adopted at the inauguration of the World Health Organization (WHO) in 1948.[5] In 2007, the American Veterinary Medical Association defined a One Health approach as ' ... the collaborative effort of multiple disciplines – working locally, nationally and globally – to attain optimal health for people, animals, and our environment'.[6]

If health is surely significant, then why is it 'One'? Is it equivalent to the population and its politics that makes health 'public'? Or is it, like in *One Medicine*, describing a tangible methodology? Who, then, is a theory of One Health for? Is it just about recognizing the essential links with nature that affect our health, or forging new connections and rebuilding bridges with natural fellows? If we can answer these questions, we might know if One Health is medicine, or public health, or something altogether different. What emerges from this Element are two ideas: one about animal rights, and one about reasonable environmentalism. Although here, these ideas are developed from afar, they tell us a great deal about the environmental challenges ahead.

2 Introduction

Zoonoses account for over half of all emerging or re-emerging diseases, many with the potential to be the next pandemic.[7] The 2009 'swine flu' pandemic should have galvanized One Health, One World, with a clear warning:

> In the final analysis, this anticlimactic pandemic might be best remembered as a trial run for the truly vicious killer that may come one day. And it has demonstrated that if influenza's Big One had struck in 2009, we would have been in a world of hurt.[8]

And yet, the 2019 COVID-19 pandemic – a 'metamorphic' socio-ecological phenomenon[9] – showed that for all that had been achieved, often fluctuating interest in pandemic preparedness mostly fell to underfunded national initiatives and these critically lacked an environmental dimension.[10] It is a story on repeat: Acquired Immune Deficiency Syndrome (AIDS) was first recognized in 1981. It started when a simian immunodeficiency virus, probably circulating in a chimpanzee (*Pan troglodytes*), infected a human being (*Homo sapiens*) somewhere in a forested area of Central Africa. That spillover was the index case for Human Immunodeficiency Virus type 1 (HIV-1). By 1984, the public health community was responding to the global crisis by linking clinical and social research. But they had identified the new disease too late; and there was a sense that opportunities had been missed that could have prevented tens of millions of deaths worldwide. There were gaps in epidemiological data, silos in practice, and hidden determinants of health driving the virus through communities. HIV would become globally endemic. If we were lucky with SARS, then COVID-19 is here to stay.

This Element is a bird's eye view. It tries to answer the question 'what is One Health?' with a general objective in mind: to prove that, in theory, it is different from other population approaches to health, and that in particular, public health responses may have a specific connotation that cannot ethically be reconciled with One Health. This Element will answer this question by analysing the systematic population problem of *interspecific justice*: a phenomenon existing or occurring between different species.[11] The probability of another pandemic is an environmental enigma: 'Disease X' – a 'pathogen currently unknown to cause human disease' – connects every natural space to communities, national interests, and development. HIV was tied to the wilderness in Africa, and SARS to animal markets in China. Swine flu originated in industrial farms in Mexico. Middle Eastern Respiratory Syndrome (MERS) started infecting humans in 2012 and has remained in that region through contact with camels (*Camelus dromedarius*); the chain of infection is still unknown. The catastrophic Western Africa Ebola outbreak in 2013 was likely due to contact with Angolan free-tailed bats (*Mops condylurus*). And then came the COVID-19 pandemic: the link to bats, again, was an indelible reminder of the connections between human health and nature.

This Element is not completed here, but it goes some way in proving that an ethical relationship with nature will reduce the risk of another pandemic, through policies that reflect the fact that we live with, work with, and care for animals. A new definition of One Health arrives much later, but it will make less sense if we skip too far and too fast forward. After all, there is more than one cause of 'our ecologically deranged planet'.[12]

I propose to search for coherency by taking a journey via three themes; these are not presented as polished surfaces but are instead arguments at different stages of research. (For One Health, there is value in study, taken step by step, amid twists and turns – bumps and potholes – of all the possible interdisciplinary paths.) The themes are as follows: historical inspirations for relating our (public) health to natural others (Section 7); the facts evident in existing human rights frameworks and the reasons for One Health emerging in international summits (Section 8); and an explanation of our ethical relationship to nature (Section 9). And to give away their relationship to one another, I suggest each theme raises questions of rights.

If these themes raise many moral issues in-and-of-themselves, I have in mind to reach only one conclusion: *One Health Environmentalism* is a response to a cultural dissonance from nature, that is impacting environmental sustainability and harms both humans and animals; that is, One Health ethics does not arise out of a *practical* – public health – concern of humans for humans, but from a lack of *theoretical* concern for animals. The climate emergencies humanity faces have mental, physical, and social impacts; these are visible as symptoms of poor health in populations, often exacerbated by injustices of social strata and circumstances in which people live and communities can be healthy. But planetary health is also affecting animals, and their health affects us in all the places we live with them. My hope, therefore, is to start a scholarly debate about radical solutions to these environmental crises, which are more difficult to gainsay in the noise of conflicting social and political agendas.

3 An(other) Environmental Crisis

One Health connects various phenomena to unhealthy environments. There are many examples.[13] Choking cities contributing to greenhouse gases; expanding and squeezing the life out of green habitats. Communities reliant on high output, monocrop fields and industrial farms that butt against and devour wilderness, leaving wastelands.[14] Biodiversity loss as irreplaceable natural resources are dug up, chopped up, and processed at an ever more alarming rate. What wilderness is left is captured by privateers, exploiting scarcity and necessity, and spitting out discernible 'public bads': the opposite of collective benefits of public goods. The plundering of ecoservices[15] 'crucial for the well-being of humans and nature',[16] often done with the main goal of simply larger profit with no end in sight; an enticement that spreads through economies of meaningless consumerism of some kind, creating vast globalized networks to extract more and more resources. Access to natural spaces becomes harder as it is rendered unsuitable for habitation; species that live there adapt, leave, or die, as it physically disappears or is privatized for personal gain. Industries take little social responsibility through shady political deals; and the goods and processes we come to rely on produce waste that become global pollutants.[17] Ignorant, corrupt, and ideological political (mis)representation, amplified by social media, contributes to social inertia, promotes populist agendas to disrupt coordinated responses, and stokes radical disobedience and then clamps down on the actions meant to protect the environment for us and future generations. These *are* existential threats: some animals – like us – can adapt their behaviour, but only we can change policies or deploy green technologies. Other species cannot evolve quickly enough; biodiversity is lost, and ecosystems transform into something far more dangerous.

Zoonoses occupy a larger space in this Element, and there is more than enough about pandemics to keep us busy here (and concerned). As well as being an area of utmost urgency,[18] pandemics, as we shall see, are a topic where the environmentalism of One Health and humanitarianism of public health are mostly in conflict, because the driving factors of zoonoses are *interspecific*, involving non-human animals and human activity in the environments we share with them. '[A]ny infectious disease is inherently an ecological system.'[19] It is in these respects that the ' ... [COVID] pandemic is no more a "natural" phenomenon than the famines of the past or the current climate crisis'.[20]

> The cumulative scientific evidence is unequivocal: climate change is a threat to human well-being and planetary health (*very high confidence*). Any further delay in concerted anticipatory global action on adaptation and mitigation will miss a brief and rapidly closing window of opportunity to secure a liveable and sustainable future for all (*very high confidence*).[21]

Anthropogenic climate trends heighten social upheaval and strife. Millions of people have been displaced; the crowded, unsafe, and unhealthy environments they end up in are ideal for spreading diseases.[22] But patterns of urbanization also create cities of concrete and tarmac ideal for resourceful animals that flourish. In places like these, uncontrolled human activity pushes ecologies to and beyond their limits, releasing latent zoonoses; new environments develop, modifying the ranges of animals that can adapt and survive, but which become test tubes for pathogen evolution and emergent diseases.[23] Deforestation causes Ebola outbreaks, industrial farming leads to swine flu, and wet markets incubate novel coronaviruses. Several diseases – such as Dengue, Zika, and Lyme – are expanding from their previous environment because of anthropogenic factors.

We already know about the next pandemic: Highly Pathogenic Avian Influenza (HPAI) was first recorded in 1997 in Hong Kong. It was linked to poultry farms and markets that turned out to be ripe for zoonotic spillover: large numbers of animals with poor welfare, species that do not normally mix in nature, in unnatural surroundings and proximity. (These conditions may also explain the origin of COVID-19: it likely started in captive animals in a Wuhan Market, kept in crowded and filthy conditions.) As well as six human deaths, the Hong Kong HPAI outbreak resulted in the 'total depopulation of all poultry markets and chicken farms'.[24] Globally, cases of HPAI or 'bird flu' (avian influenza A, paralytically subtypes H5N1, H7N9, and H3N8) are becoming more common in wild and farmed birds, thought to involve migrating birds as well as human movement and trade. Human infection is rare, but for those who catch it, around 60 per cent die, making it a potential pandemic many magnitudes more deadly than COVID-19. HPAI has been found in domestic dogs, foxes (family *Canidae*), bobcats (family *Felidae*), skunks (family *Mephitidae*), raccoons (family *Procyonidae*), bears (family *Ursidae*), otters and minks (family *Mustelidae*), seals and sea lions (families *Phocidae* and *Otariidae*). In October 2022, H5N1 was found in farmed mink in Spain.[25] It was an alarming discovery, because it was evident of inter-mammalian infections; and although no human-to-human infection has been detected yet, that would be the first sign of an imminent pandemic.

Given that bird flu is endemic in nature, how do we prepare for (it as) the next pandemic? In the case of bird flu, international conventions protect migrating birds as they pass through different jurisdictions, so that source of spread cannot be easily contained by traditional means. Public health relies on surveillance, track and trace. Once the alarm is raised, we rely on responses such as quarantine, but only for humans; all other animals risk being culled. To date, millions of captive and wild birds have been infected and have died; many more of them are intentionally slaughtered.

The ecological and geographical global reality is that nature traverses political borders; it frames the world as ethically 'porous',[26] justifying an approach to understand ' . . . both human and non-human indices of health, and the wider study of biospheres, ecosystems, and "social" networks'.[27] While the second part of this claim suggests a One Health 'approach' (Section 4.1), there has been less willingness in the field to address practical trade-offs that might be necessary for environmental fairness or justice. So I want to move back a few steps and focus this Element on a specific purpose: to undertake an ethical analysis of One Health as ' . . . a process of constructing a shared understanding of the evidential basis for neglected and critical ethical problems that call for structural change'.[28]

4 Methodology

Keeping this Element within a manageable scope, which is original, succinct, and authoritative, is a challenge with two areas as big as public health and environmentalism. This Methodology is much longer than I hoped, but while preparing the ground, I realized that it could have been a (fourth) theme: a story of the struggle to find relevance for a 'new' idea. For my purposes, I merely clear some underbrush, rather than risk taking byways that extend this Element to unconscionable length.

So, to keep this enquiry on track, this Element does not cover many theories of environmentalism and does not circle back to the principles of animal ethics in detail. Also, you will not find many 'One Health' cases discussed in depth. Only at the end do I give some ideas for ethical implementation (Section 10), but this is mostly about inspiring further thoughts. It is also not my place to try to improve on public health ethics. Before saying anything more, let me make it clear that this Element does not set out to undermine the purposes of public health; it is not a choice of either public health or One Health. I also forewarn the reader that I shall be giving each of the three themes – history, law, ethics – a slant that favours philosophical ways of thinking, and by-passing others.

The thematic approach involves transitions from historical, through legal, and eventually a bioethical method, as though they were interlinked. I anticipate that some readers will view this method with suspicion: what has *this* author accomplished here, in expanding methods in history, legal theory, and bioethics? There are indeed nuances to every methodology, including understanding their limitations.[29] But there are already different methodological assumptions in One Health practice we should be aware – that is at the core of any kind of practical disciplinarity, after all. So each of the following themes is only meant to give a flavour of three kinds of systematic enquiry, and to organize discourse around the significance of each: the historical origins of One Health, its appearance in international law, and its ethical foundations, should stand together to justify both my course and destination.

I will now take a moment to say a few words about definitions. Firstly, all possibilities for the concepts used are not cited; earlier drafts that did so, became unwieldy. Some of the terms I have already used – among others, *anthropocentric, culture, nature* – are notoriously fuzzy and each one could take up the entirety of a volume in the Cambridge University Press Elements series. As such, I do not want to be bogged down in semantics and particularities, so I will be general in my treatment of things like economics, and some suspended assumptions will be necessary for the sake of brevity. For instance, my use of law throughout is simplified as it relates to the international bodies we already have (in particular, the United Nations); I will not address in fine detail jurisprudential controversies, specific places of law, or instances of legislation. International fora have become the basis for conventions on biodiversity and climate accords and use the language of human rights. Rights will be the primary topic in theme three.

I use a few conventions: (non-human) *animals* to distinguish between *human* (beings) and other species (recognizing that humans are primates, mammals, etc.). 'Species' is not an easy concept. Here, I use species generally to mean a natural taxonomic unit, even though the rules are not discrete. Individuals within each species have different capacities, and there are commonalities, that is, all mammals require air; all vertebrate species are sentient; all Great Apes 'think'. (This is fundamental to theme three, too.)

The meaning of disciplinary and specific technical terms are not always given in this Element, so some basic scientific understanding is assumed. For example, a *spillover* can be defined as the cross-species transmission of a pathogen into a host population not previously infected. But it is a complex and multifactorial phenomenon, involving aspects associated with the biology and genetics of the host, reservoir, vector, and microorganisms involved, and the environmental context. *Zoonoses* spread to humans by direct contact, from food or water, fomites or environmental contamination; humans infect animals with *zooanthroponoses*. There is also the technical language about contextual relations on the land, water, or between flora and fauna – and every location and species found, infers countless researches in biology, ecology, genomics, and many others, that connect ecosystems to the biosphere.

Since I am making conceptual comparisons, I will do away with one health as a proper noun, to match the convention for naming public health, ecology, and conservation.

4.1 A One Health Approach

The methodological steps taken here are necessary if only to avoid what Robert Merton called 'The Fallacy of the Latest Word', and the risk that 'wholesale neglect of theoretical contexts soon fall of their own weight'.[30] If these remarks suggest that one health has become a nominalist fallacy – a generalization that fails to explain exactly what it *is* – then to leave the matter thus is to leave it vague and obscure. My other motivation is Stephen Jay Gould's opus, *The Structure of Evolutionary Theory*, in which he claims, 'Theories need both essences and histories.'[31] I think we can borrow from this an entirely appropriate abstract anchor to try to solve the puzzle of what connects us to nature: in theory, then, is there an intrinsic quality to one health? Is it, like evolutionary theory (taking on Gould's challenge), a 'genuine thing'?[32]

The following investigation reveals that there is a tension *within* one health. A keynote speaker at the One Health–One World symposium, WCS President Steven Sanderson described the consequences of globalization as '[rescuing] conservation from development[,] and poverty alleviation from ecological degradation'.[33] In theory and in fact, ' ... two claims are simultaneously true: there is a threat to the human life support at the same time as several billions of fellow humans have to be lifted out of poverty'.[34] So, if the gist of both one health and public health concerns the same scale of populations and same determinants of health,[35] then why cannot public health do the ethical work?

Public health outcomes, which are measured in terms of social and environmental justice, might include an approach to 'maintain ... culture ... for the broader public good'.[36] How does social justice relate to nature or wilderness, and the lives of animals that live there: *what is good for them*?

And so I distinguish between one health *ethics* and a one health *approach*. The one health approach gives a name to something far from new, yet it has become a focal point to encourage people to talk with those they would not normally think to do so: it meant to be multidisciplinary, interdisciplinary, or transdisciplinary – which suggests at least it is not simply uni-disciplinary. However, an approach gives a weak semblance of purpose between those heading in the same direction, whereas ethics indicates a common value – a purpose for the journey.

Inter- and transdisciplinary approaches, developed in the social sciences, have become theory-derived conceptual guides for justifying empirical support for one health. But though there is perhaps modern significance in holism, methodologically speaking at least, it is a long time since social-scientific phenomena were thought to be completely explicable in terms of individual disciplines. Moreover, these theories often lack ecological relevance.[37] In respect to the socio-economic expectations for transdisciplinarity,[38] the approach is as much about convergence in terms of coming together on what we agree about, as well as amalgamating different disciplines, practices, and agencies; achieving that goal presupposes a normative, coordinating principle. However, the one health approach itself does not extend what might be the 'right theory' into diverse areas of practice, and fails to provide a critique perhaps needed, particularly in respect to the divergent values of economics, public health, ecology, and conservation. The problem of an approach, therefore, is that it tells us little about thematic critique: the destinations of history, law, or ethics.

That said, an approach can have tacit importance: in the following, where sources on public health, conservation, or ecology, are cited, the authors or their words are meant – in the spirit of the approach – to be authentic and authoritative, as if we were at a multidisciplinary meeting, *à la*: 'At every step, in order to visualize the consequences, we need to go through some laboratories to learn new techniques, to be confident in the results of some instruments, and to appeal to some experts.'[39]

Joël de Rosnay used the idea of *The Macroscope* (1979) to refocus our gaze outwards from society to nature – a 'symbolic instrument made of a number of methods and techniques borrowed from very different disciplines';[40] this, too, will be used to navigate the great distance I have to cross to find a common one health vocabulary.

4.2 Environments, Cultures, and Natures

Everything we do is situated in some sort of environment (*environ*, from Old French of 'round about', to surround or encircle). Thomas Carlyle first coined the term 'environment' in English, although the path to its association with 'nature' and then environmentalism would take more time. But has there ever been a more slippery concept than *nature*?[41] *Nature* is wondrous, perhaps with objective, naturalistic, or sometimes fallacious value; it can have rights (assertorically – the fact of natural rights), or it can be unfeeling and harsh (teleologically speaking). Yet organisms have the specific natures of their species, and some have fluctuating capabilities of reason. So nature also prompts specific kinds of rights discourse, including the issue of whether (and which) animals have rights, that manifest in a growing jurisprudence to recognize the legal claims of natural objects such as rivers. With such limitless parentheses, the risk is too much to do; so, here, although 'the environment' and 'nature' have perhaps different connotations, I rest assured that there cannot be one without the other: it would seem there are few places *in* nature where humans have not been (our traces can be found everywhere), and it is impossible to keep nature *from* the artificial worlds we build. As such, I will use environment and nature interchangeably.

And what do I mean by *culture*? That is another impossibly difficult word to pin down; but we need a placeholder. For the most part, here I use nature as the opposite of *culture*[42] – how we subjectively see it the environment in respect to all the necessary ecoservices or the things humans need to be healthy. (Not forgetting that ecological services are nature's goods and are necessary, contextual, and relational, to all animals.) Sometimes culture is seen as an object of human making, of art or language, and is seen as essentially separate from the non-human world.[43] That is, culture is responsible for the wondrous signs all around us of *human* intellectual achievements and spiritual imaginations;[44] it is the evolutionary endpoint of ultra-sociality, such that institutions of economies, ethics, and law, cannot be found in nature.[45] Culture is therefore thought to be anthropo*genic* (*anthrōpos*, 'human being'; -*genic*, as in origin or cause), in the sense that we 'think' and behave like humans, rather than, as Aldo Leopold wrote, like 'a Mountain'.[46] Many animals *are* social and cultural;[47] they just do not have things like books or tactical nukes. And perhaps they do think like *us*, which is only to say that their plausible consciousness pertains to certain neuroethical facts.[48]

The significance of culture and nature will become more apparent: the law (in theme two), for instance, uses a blanket concept of *legal persons* to focus a social concern and avoid such thorny matters of natural rights;[49] but, as we shall see, that approach gets in a muddle if there are in fact natural persons. Moreover, that approach suggests to me a hint of chauvinism[50] and hubris – 'look, at *us*! Look at what *we've* achieved! We have left nature behind!' I have instead a foreboding – philosophical – sense of what humanity is capable of. (Compare Calvin Schwabe, an architect of One Medicine, who wrote sympathetically of the obligations of a culture that ' . . . *is* more important than animals'.[51]) So the concerns of what we leave out by *being* anthropo*centric*, or, if you believe there is a metaphysical *dis*connection, then one health's modern revelations are reasons for positive environmental health reform by recognizing mutuality or a one-ness of health.

4.3 Ecology and Conservation

In 1866, the zoologist Ernst Haeckel first defined the new science of 'Oecologie'. His idea is translated in the front matter to the major modern work, *Principles of Animal Ecology*: 'By ecology we mean the body of know-ledge concerning the economy of nature – the investigation of the total relations of the animal both to its inorganic and to its organic environment; . . . in a word, ecology is the study of all those complex interrelations referred to by Darwin as the conditions of the struggle for existence.'[52]

Arthur Tansley, a pioneer in botany, used *ecology* for the first time in 1935 (*eco* – From Greek *oikos* meaning 'household', home, or place to live), to mean studying 'ecosystems' *as they are*: 'If human activity destroys a large number of plant communities and plant habitats, and modifies, to a greater or less extent, many more, it also produces fresh habitats and fresh plant communities, and thus provides fresh opportunities for ecological study on every hand.'[53]

Later came a revelation in social environmental ideas, based on the field study of natural organisms under natural conditions, with 'natural' taken to mean 'non-human'. In this ideal sense, ecology became the antithesis to culture, requiring the 'protection of nature from human obliteration'.[54] A fourth strand concerns the fact that the relative instability of ecosystems was significant: as they could change suddenly due to a natural seismic event, there was a value to 'unnatural' and synthetic systems never before in existence.[55] The molecular biologist Joël De Rosnay seems to be the first to have coined 'ecohealth':

> 'Ecosocialism, ecosociety, ecocitizen, ecocommunications, ecohealth, ecocongress . . . This is not a new 'ecocult'! The prefix 'eco' symbolizes here the close relationship between economy and ecology; it puts the accent on relationships among [persons] and between [persons] and what they call their 'home,' the ecosphere.'[56]

The ideas of ecology, therefore, were shaped by the contingent realities of overcoming environmental problems through 'systems thinking' about humans living in world of infinite complexity: ecology could not be separated from economy, urban planning, and industry.

Wildlife conservation can be both naturalistic (the observation and recording of nature, as a scientific interest) and specialistic (the conservation of species – and spaces). But both community-based conservation and social ecology – a commentary on the phases of study just mentioned – seem to have landed in the same place: a combination of an anthropocentric or *humanist* concern for human beings and the value of nature that originates in human interest, *and* a view through *naturalistic* lenses that discerns environmental value autonomously of the human gaze. The latter includes biocentric and ecocentric views that, respectively, consider animals or the environment has intrinsic interests.

Even though my treatment ends up leaving these as bite-size concepts, they tell us a great deal about one health: understanding ecological communities requires contributions from biologists, conservationists, ecologists, ethologists, geneticists, microbiologists, and so on, as well as historians, legal scholars, philosophers, and sociologists. But that approach also tells us that combining such views into one of culture *and* nature is an ethical project.

4.4 Public Health

Perhaps there is a glaring omission on my part: I so far have not said what 'one' and 'health' mean. Although I give a definition of one health ethics, that is a long way away. (It is given in Section 9, if the present reader seeks urgent satisfaction.) There is much distance to cross, including (as we shall see) two potential dead ends. For now, I anticipate the scope of the task I have set myself; it is hard enough to define 'health' even when taking a single, intraspecies frame about human beings. An interspecies approach only amplifies these.

So my assumption is purposively simple: I use *public* to relate to human communities, and assume it has an anthropocentric meaning based on the idea that 'human culture', and it alone, has absolute and unconditional value.

A great deal has been written about the question: *what is health*? *Health* is a description of well-being if taken at the level of an abstract individual. But it is also a contextual and shared state, central to public health ethics. *Public health* has been defined as many things, often by focussing on what the public *is* and how that relates to *its* health (John Coggon writes that, in all this variation, there may not be a 'true' meaning in what makes health public).[57] Nevertheless, in the broadest sense, 'When public health talks about health it means a state of biological, psychological, and social functioning of a human organism/person in a social context';[58] this social turn was not always seen as important from a population health perspective.[59] (And is perhaps similar to the social evolution of ecology and conservation, discussed in Section 4.3.) I use public health to describe the traditional science and art to improve well-being, applicable only to 'legal persons' – and that means human beings – and the communities in which they live.

'One' now seems pivotal. Both one health and public health are similar in respect to 'how to think about the nature of the health of the group and how this differs from the health of individuals',[60] and share the imperative to improve welfare by leveraging social opportunities and evidence-based approaches to design better systems. But if public health is coextensive to *human* rights – a recurring subplot of this Element – then one health differs insomuch as it *includes* animals in moral decisions, and therefore does not contain exactly the same *humanistic* values.

5 A Natural Condition

If we can entertain the idea that one health *is* interspecific, then its contrast with public health might illuminate a different evidence-based theory. The risk I am taking is making public health and one health practically incompatible, perpetually in conflict, and rendering public health itself exposed to the logical demands of environmental ethics. But my analysis is aimed at a narrow area of public health *theory*, since merely negative criticism of the entire practice seems out of place.

Late in 2013, a new Zaire Ebolavirus strain emerged in Guinea, West Africa. It might have started when a two-year-old boy encountered locally roosting bats.[61] The WHO declared the outbreak to be an international public health emergency in August 2014.[62] By the time it was brought under control in 2016, there had been 28,652 reported cases and 11,325 deaths; many who survived infection had debilitating comorbidities. Ebola disease was first scientifically identified in 1976; over the years several local spillovers have occurred when encountering infected animals; and anthropogenic environmental factors, like deforestation, seemed to increase risks.[63] The scale of the West Africa outbreak – the largest in recorded history – was the consequence of infections reaching large urban centres for the first time.[64] It was exacerbated by the circumstances of already beleaguered public health systems in the region; their dire state – a 'clinical desert' – was symptomatic of a history of 'rapacious extraction', regional patterns of land use, and instability with roots in colonialism.[65] Political and social conflict had eroded the regional infrastructure for water, sanitation, transportation, health services, and communications needed to effectively respond. Although there must have been a causal human–ecological interaction that defined a primary spillover event, ' . . . that doesn't mean that human-animal contact defines epidemics, which occur among and between people'.[66] In this space, we find *public health ethics*.[67]

Animals rarely receive the benefits of public health-informed care.[68] In the context of public health emergencies, the focus is on human cases first, then on the social contexts of spread;[69] the ecology of hosts and reservoirs are secondary studies,[70] and there is (by some) little regard at the time for wildlife conservation. But in these same environments, populations of chimpanzees (*Pan troglodytes*) and gorillas (*Gorilla gorilla*) have been decimated by Ebola viruses, as well as by other human activities, and their population resilience is at critically low levels. Vaccines were only preclinical at the start of the Ebola outbreak, leading to 'ethical and evidential grounds' to test them in humans likely to be exposed to the virus.[71] The experimental use of the vaccine in humans raised questions of 'compassionate use' and regulatory issues under the umbrella of the WHO's public health remit. The vaccines were urgently tested in non-human primate models, but if the human trials went ahead, then could they not concurrently serve as a model for Great Ape vaccination programmes, too?[72] Perhaps our closest cousins could benefit from data gleaned from human trials, and then the outcomes of vaccinations *in situ* could have informed public health. For some conservationists, 'interventions such as vaccination and treatment remain controversial'.[73] Vaccination programmes aimed at wild, rare, socially important animals are presumed to be unworkable or too risky. But it was the very high stakes vaccine 'experiment' – lacking the normal range of pre-clinical animal experiments – that got us out of COVID-19.

Within nature, therefore, are ethical patterns of politics and sociality: these narratives can explain the links between zoonoses and society,[74] just as much as culture defines matters within the frame of public health.

5.1 One Health and COVID-19

'HUMAN BEINGS ARE THE ULTIMATE CAUSES OF PANDEMICS . . . [O]ur growing ecological footprint seems currently to be leading to an exponential rise in the spillover of other microbes directly from wildlife to people'.[75]

As the COVID-19 pandemic entered its third year, a British health minister was recorded in interview saying '[at the start of the pandemic] there was an idea at one moment that we might have to ask the public to exterminate all the cats in Britain'. The open revelation, made only because of leaked private messages (and perhaps, ironically was meant as a distracting 'dead cat' strategy), was said to be justified at that time by limited data about the virus and the risks of non-human animals being infected. In China's zero-COVID policy, companion animals were forcibly seized and placed together in plastic bags to be collected at the roadside, and killed in large numbers because they were potentially infected with (or thought to be spreading) the virus. Around the world, wild animals such as deer were killed because of the risk of spreading the virus, even though that risk was much lower than catching it from another human being.

For all the other matters these stories represent, they also do not seem to be reasonable. Even though the origin of the virus was unknown at the time, it was a characteristic zoonoses; and now it had become a zooanthroponoses: humans were shedding the virus and infecting animals. Not all non-human species could carry the virus, and few seemed to get seriously ill. Some zoo-kept animals were inoculated using one of the meant-for-human vaccines. Mink (genus *Mustela*) farms became incubators for new COVID-19 variants: industrial farming required close contact between large numbers of solitary animals that would never occur in the wild. In November 2020, it was announced that all farmed mink in Denmark would be culled; not just those infected or known to be exposed to the virus. Denmark's Foreign Minister said, 'We would rather go a step too far than take a step too little to combat COVID-19'. The political fallout from the decision, including its economic impact on the fur industry, contributed to the government's collapse. At the time, the WHO advised that: 'This event highlights the important role that farmed mink populations can play in the on-going transmission of SARS-CoV-2 and the critical importance of robust surveillance, sampling and sequencing of these viruses by employing a One Health approach, especially around areas where such animal reservoirs are identified.'[76]

Mink culls happened elsewhere; but the political and public debate had nothing much to do with nature and was mostly about 'the public interest'. The sight of the decaying mink re-emerging from mass graves was a reminder of the ethical discord between public health and environmentalism.

Culling is a basic tool of pandemic response; a 'stamping out' strategy to deal with an outbreak,[77] even if more humane and potentially more effective alternatives exist such as vaccination.[78] Ethically, this signifies the difference between ethical populations: humans and animals.[79] The re-emergence of SARS in 2004 led to the culling of civet cats and other mammals in China. In Singapore, preparing for future pandemics included trials of practice culls of healthy birds on the island.[80] In the United Kingdom, a mostly useless and scientifically flawed badger cull was trialled and continued beyond knowing its failure to control bovine tuberculosis (which is not a significant health risk for humans).[81] Animal populations may be 'hunted' if they escape captivity, and 'depopulated' if they are generally unwanted. If they are in danger from natural disasters, social unrest, or war (also all relatable to patterns of infectious disease), it might not be possible or popular for them to be evacuated or relocated, leading them to die in desperate conditions or 'humanely' killed. During the Ebola outbreak in Western Africa, Spanish officials euthanized a companion dog, called Excalibur. Doing so not only wasted a life, but also exacerbated the trauma and grief for their human companion, a nurse who contracted the disease from patients she was treating while in Sierra Leone. Javier Limon Romero was quarantined and received care; Excalibur was killed because there were no protocols or resources in place to care for the animal given the potential risk to public health.

Meanwhile, nature outside our windows seemed to improve while we were confined to our homes to avoid contact with the SARS-CoV-2 virus (if we were lucky enough to have a home). If these were the 'environmental "benefits" during this period ... [how could these] be celebrated for anything other than their circumstantial occurrence at a time when people are dying and coming to terms with the personal and socioeconomic effects of a global pandemic'.[82] The 'anthropause' also revealed wildlife had adapted to our day-to-day activity in more normal times, such as finding less road kill on now empty byways.[83] It also showed the necessary attachment we have to the outside: at the start, in some places, parks were closed keeping us penned in; then we were isolated in green belt or concrete neighbourhoods. More companion animals were bought or adopted to keep us company; but if staying home was not to be the new normal, then the return to offices eroded a responsibility for their care. Of course, the great social and moral reset never came, partly because of the economic recovery was seeded exactly as before.

Only now are we coming to the realization that we are all connected to a distant market in Wuhan: 'Society has long since moved beyond the narrow confines of the social sphere.'[84] Instead of dissonance to the plight of the animals in the market, there is now an unwelcome correlation between them, humanity, and a virus. If one health relates to culture and nature, then just as much, it concerns the tension between public health and conservation. These dichotomies might originate in the same places, but they are just under the surface, and hard to make out. Emerging into the post-COVID world, such obscurity is revealed as social (the reality that we live with other creatures), biological (the facts of life, so that we cannot prove we are the *only* creatures with interests), and ecological (we cannot imagine a world without a sky and land, even in the synthetic or artificial places we construct). The biosphere, on which we naturally depend, connects us *to* and *in* environments, even to the most distant of places. We can't just concrete over and eliminate nature as a way out of that fact; it makes things worse, and ultimately imperils our own existence.

6 Three Themes

In a paradigmatic one health case, the ethical concerns of public health and animal welfare were tested qualitatively in controlling rabies (*Lyssavirus*) in Colombo City, Sri Lanka.[85] The project's application of 'one health' methods (such as vaccination, addressing dog ownership responsibilities, and reducing roaming dog nuisances), suggested the approach was effective – one health decreased human infections and reduced public bads when compared to traditional policies of capture and culling. The researchers also showed that one health forces us to re-evaluate ethical assumptions: instead of dead dogs, there were educated owners and healthy canines, and tangible collective goods in public awareness, animal welfare, and safer environments. The positive results, however, could not fully explain the role of ethics: the investigators asked, were the dogs (genus *Canis*) being respected, treated fairly, or attributed rights? And what if there were conflicts as a result of these measures? Specific answers might not matter, as the case showed that one health can work at a population level without defining it as an ethical solution; but populations contain people with rights, and the public good and the public interest might do the ethical work to resolve conflicts between them, but do little for animals.

To make sense of moral connection to nature, some have turned back to public health and its implied normativity.[86] Similarly to the Columbo case, we can trace human/animal connections to many different matters (In Section 5, I used the examples like vaccinating great apes to Ebola, or the environmental framing of COVID-19). But across these cases, perhaps one health itself has first principles – is there, in this case, an imperative to vaccinate rather than cull? Does one health in principle suggest that great apes, dogs, or other animals have rights? And given these possibilities, does that make one health cases more appealing or undermine central population health dogma?

In an attempt to answer these, theme one reveals an incomplete origin story for one health; as such, there is an alternative history – one about theory – which may tell us something, but perhaps not enough, about relevant schools of environmental ethics. If that process does not do well, then we can move on to the fora for environmental law where one health has been stationed, to perhaps find answers (that is theme two; although I do not find it convincing, either); and ultimately, perhaps we might seek out more solid philosophical grounding that befits an ethical theory (theme three).

7 Theme One: One Health's Ethical Histories

What follows, is a shorter, but critical story about how one health evolved as a social history.[87] My method is limited: as we move a matter back and forward in logical sequence, each step echoes with knowledge, discoveries, movements, and controversies, and so, each footprint resonates with almost infinite interpretations. But a short history is, nonetheless, an opportunity to understand intuitive leaps, false starts, and mistakes, and to tie up loose ends. In this theme, the subplot is to anticipate a theoretical frame sneaking, without critique, its way into the 'newly' discovered idea of one health. The account is in rough chronological order; no character mentioned is treated biographically (birth and death dates are included to place them in the period); and no institution described in full context.

7.1 One Medicine

The idea of nature goes far back beyond pre-modern philosophy, religion, and tradition. One could probably make the case that the idea of one health, too, can be found in all ancient medicine: cultivation, hunting, and husbandry, always meant that animals were perceived in places that were connected to our well-being and often cared for.[88] Aggrey Ayuen Majok (1947–2020) and Calvin Schwabe (1927–2006) describe three social systems related to animal roles: folk, agrarian, and industrian.[89] At the furthest end, animals are completely integrated culturally and economically within social fabric, whereas at the other, there is a culture mostly disconnected from nature. In Western narratives, one health history zooms in on the last 250 years and professes to find only a crumbling human relationship to the environment and mentions a few bright sparks who cared to notice. In this story, and surely there must be many, One Medicine is part of the Microbiological Revolution, development of faultless microscopes, and progress in cell theory. But it is also during this time that urbanization, social stratification on an industrial scale, exploration and exploitation of far-off places, and ever larger wars, meant living with animals in increasingly unhealthy conditions and proximity meant sharing germs with similar pathologies, aetiologies, and outcomes. New work for (and exploitation of) animals necessitated growth in the profession of veterinary medicine to keep them well; and such communal experiences became part of the environmental hygiene and sanitary causes of ill health (later public health).

It was the American physician Benjamin Rush (1746–1813) who first said on record, 'There is but one medicine . . . and there is but one animal, because every animal is a living creature, or at least an automaton . . .'.[90] Rush taught medical students about society's collective obligations to animals '. . . by the manner of life to which their connexion with us . . .',[91] 'We are bound in the first place, to discharge the important duties to domestic animals which I have mentioned, by the relation that has been established between them and us by the Author of nature . . .',[92] and in particular, of 'the reciprocal advantages to be derived from extending to them, the benefits of the science of medicine'.[93] Such obligations were derived from service and companionship, 'They live only for our benefit . . . so that there is constantly due, to them, an immense balance of debt from us ...'.[94] One Medicine particularly found a place in pathology: Rudolf Virchow (1821–1902)[95] was said to have first laid the groundwork – he was also first to note that 'all cells come from cells' – which would eventually become a grounded theory: 'I can only emphasize once more that there is no scientific barrier, nor should there be, between veterinary medicine and human medicine; the experience of one must be utilized for the development of the other.'[96]

A contemporary of Virchow, William Osler (1849–1919), continued that heritage: '"ills which flesh is heir to" are not wholly monopolized by the "lords of creation"'.[97]

Although a straight-line is drawn between these élites and one health, there are only fragments of ethical thinking to connect them. Admittedly, I have not attempted textbook coverage because these were times of celebrated literati, each with a vast preserve of discoveries, experiments, ideas, travels, and correspondences. Rush was perhaps an outlier – he considered there to be obligations whether treating disease in humans or animals – but, as reported by a contemporary, he was criticized by his peers for suggesting that human 'souls' must perish, like *all* animals, with the disintegration of the body.[98] (The controversy brings to mind Gregor Mendel's (1822–1884) fear of 'many clerical enemies'.[99]) For others, One Medicine only bound humans to animals through studying the diseases they shared; medicine informed forms of germinal ideas of interdisciplinarity between veterinary and clinical colleges, rather than playing any part in pioneering trans-professional ethical values. In those times, (Cartesian) dualism always was just under the surface. Virchow wrote of the Theory of Evolution, 'We cannot teach, we cannot pronounce it to be a conquest of science, that man has descended from any other animal.'[100] Osler was familiar with the works of Darwin (and met him once, in 1874), but although he transformed his religious idealism into progressive social medicine and advocated for better living conditions, he, at least for a large part of his career, was reluctant to forego his concerns about the new Theory.[101] Both Virchow and Osler were pro-vivisection. Virchow thought animal research to be in the 'public weal' and assured readers of the *British Medical Journal* that no one was after 'pet dogs, and parlour cats'.[102] Osler formally spoke against the British government's intention to introduce The Cruelty to Animals Act 1876, which would restrict painful experiments. He gave evidence regarding the ' ... tremendous gain to humanity ... that it is impossible to put against it the lives of a certain number of dogs sacrificed. I do not think that the two can be weighed together'.[103]

In the twentieth century, the One Medicine idea grew under new public health policies. In 1923, Veranus Moore (1859–1931, principally a bacteriologist) wrote 'We are coming to realize that, broadly speaking, there is but one medicine; and that physicians and veterinarians alike are obligated to safeguard the public health.'[104] In 1958, Joseph Klauder (1888–1962, a dermatologist), credited Virchow (without proper citation) as saying 'There is no dividing line in nature of disease of man and animals.'[105] Klauder saw promise in another concept of 'universal medicine':[106] a concern for the health of all living creatures, that 'is simply the result of that obsolete concept of division: Man and Animal'.[107] In 1964, in *Veterinarians and What They Do*, a chapter proclaims, 'There is only one medicine' (and that 'could well be the title of the book').[108] The authors' narrative refers to Rush's first utterance to allude to the veterinarians' role in public health.[109] In 1966, One Medicine was used to define 'a decade on preparing for human travel in space . . .',

> . . . as far as the cerebral circulation is concerned, the effect is the same as if a man had become a giraffe. This problem was a major reason for applying the One Medicine idea to a study of the giraffe's circulation. . . . and that man's physiological weaknesses will be supported so effectively by the One Medicine of Mother Earth that he will be able to travel to the moon and eventually to other planets. What he will find there remains to be seen, but his experiences undoubtedly will make important additions to our One Medicine.[110]

The concept of One Medicine again appeared in 1975, in respect to using a 'baboon heart to support a critically ill child': 'Thus the concept of 'one medicine' grows, and the boundary between the twin disciplines of human and animal medicine becomes increasingly blurred.'[111]

Despite these earlier articulations of One Medicine, the veterinary epidemiologist Calvin Schwabe is often credited with establishing the practice in modern parlance. Schwabe was moved by the relationships between medical and agricultural practices in prehistoric and classical societies, and came to the conclusion 'that veterinary medicine was important for human public health, and that there should be a legitimate space for veterinarians to contribute to that goal'.[112] He decided that 'Virchow from the start became completely dedicated to the idea of "one medicine"' (citing Klauder's rendition).[113] A version of Virchow's prose appeared on the front plate of the first edition of Schwabe's seminal book, *Veterinary Medicine and Human Health* (1964). But it was not until the third edition, published in 1984, that he included a chapter on 'One Medicine'.[114] Here, he calls One Medicine a 'human health profession',[115] defined by 'the most logical unifying or apical cause in veterinary medicine's hierarchy of values'[116] with the 'same dimensions and general goals of medicine',[117] that extends the treatment of disease *to all species* as 'shared experiences'.[118] Schwabe promoted the veterinary profession as a *means* to human well-being, which meant looking after animals well. Later, Schwabe declared that 'One Medicine for the Future' meant veterinary preventative medicine was fundamental to public health.[119] With others, he developed epidemiological surveillance research in respect to population-based health using a 'web of causation' between animals and humans;[120] that opened up a 'two-way window' for interprofessional interactions,[121] and described multiple etiological environmental determinants. This determinant of health vision was necessary because holistic approaches were rare in a public health movement that was becoming increasingly focused on the chronic and non-infectious diseases of human populations.

At around the same time One Medicine entered the mid-to-late twentieth-century lexicon, two 'new' environmental movements came to prominence: EcoHealth and Planetary Health. I hesitate to say much more of their history as they are more often conflated across a spectrum of approaches including global health. In that respect, these concepts, as well as one health and One Medicine, are often used interchangeably. But perhaps I can make some simple observations if only to put them *in name* to one side.

Ecohealth – or ecological health – at one point was a field of study about people's quality of life as it is embedded in healthy communities; since then, the concept has oscillated between well-being movements and conservation medicine.

> Both ecohealth and public health aspire at social equity through healthy societies, and share strategies for community participation and empowerment for the solution of health problems. ... Public health is traditionally considered the responsibility of the state; whereas, ecohealth stresses the involvement of communities and seems to have (maybe out of frustration) relegated the role of the state to second place in the solution of the problems.[122]

Conservation medicine professes to offer sustainable ways to use wildlife by engaging veterinarians in improving social and economic factors.[123] The EcoHealth Alliance (which started as the Wildlife Trust in 1971) has since become synonymous with approaches to preventing human pandemics that start in animals.

The Rockefeller Foundation-Lancet Commission on Planetary Health (2015) stated, 'Put simply, planetary health is the health of human civilization and the state of the natural systems on which it depends.'[124] It has since manifested as a critique of political, economic, and social systems, largely contained in institutions (like hospitals), and linking them to the climate crisis.[125]

These are now non-reductionist models of population health that take account of various contextual factors – or social and environmental determinants of health – to bring communities under ' ... the normative demands of justice as they relate to the activities of public health policy, practice, and research'.[126]

Both movements are synonymous with meeting the United Nation's *Sustainable Development Goals*: a 'new set of SDGs should ensure that human societies operate within the safe operating space defined by planetary boundaries'.[127] I am not generally critical of the global movement to connect environmentalism to the planetary crisis, but as we shall see, if that is grounded in public health (as it must be), then there are inevitable conflicts with nature.

7.2 From One Medicine to One Health

The '"one medicine, many ecosystems" approach to protecting livelihoods, [and] addressing poverty and environmental issues' was still evident at the turn of the twenty-first century.[128] But at this point, there was also a shift towards something called 'one health'. Conservationists had noticed a tension; William Karesh, a veterinarian, wrote 'I cannot accept the argument that conservation puts animals before people. . . . Many of our needs to survive in the future are similar.'[129] Karesh gave this germinal idea a name in 2003 (sounding like Benjamin Rush): 'There is just one health. And the solutions require everyone working together on all the different levels.'[130]

One health was going to be a theme at the upcoming *Southern and East African Experts Panel on Designing Successful Conservation and Development Interventions at the Wildlife/Livestock Interface* forum (2003). Participants would be told, 'As socioeconomic progress demands sustained improvements in health for humans, their domestic animals, and the environment, our institutions recognize the need to move towards a "one health" perspective.'[131]

The perspective was confirmation of what had been happening for a while: 'conservation biologists have the opportunity to identify more interdisciplinary barriers needing removal and to construct bridges to connect castles of disciplinary knowledge'.[132] Like Schwabe's veterinarians, conservationists had for a long time understood practical reasons to connect public health to the environment: the primatologist Jane Goodall had already published observations of natural disease transmission.[133] And in this respect, 'The veterinary expertise and wildlife management skills of conservation organizations can both supplement the basic pathogen research and control work of the public health community and benefit from it.'[134]

Across the board, conservationists were already studying not just the biological and evolutionary factors of animal diseases, but also the complex 'social' ecology in which humans become a part of the natural life cycles. That idea would become mythological in the burgeoning one health movement.

The 'new' one health would be a reminder that naturalist skills were rarely used in public health.

In 2004, one health was formally defined (see the opening of this Element). The definition included *The Manhattan Principles on One World, One Health* organized around 'interdisciplinary and cross-sectoral approaches to disease prevention, surveillance, monitoring, control and mitigation as well as to environmental conservation more broadly'.[135] Now, one health had a focus: a response to future epidemics and epizootic disease risks, and in particular the concerns of international animal trade and the lack of investment in animal surveillance. Human diseases were linked to the conservation of animals already under threat; health was cyclical between species; so there was an undeniable connection between *our health*.

In 2005, Steven Osofsky et al. wrote: 'The "One Health" concept takes conservation medicine a step further by broadening an ecological definition of health, while acknowledging that conservation medicine's primary goal is the pursuit of ecological health – the health of ecosystems and the species that live within these systems.'[136]

That might have been a coda to the first phase of one health, because things then began to change, as the idea moved away from conservation into health promotion and closer to public health.[137] At least one path taken meant dropping even implied interspecific values, and adapting to a global health ethics of '... development, international health, aid and post-colonial reconstruction'.[138] Subsequent to the *New Delhi International Ministerial Conference on Avian and Pandemic Influenza* in 2007, the Food and Agriculture Organization (FAO) with other major global organizations published their *Contributing to One World, One Health*, a significant reiteration for global action in respect to 'infectious diseases that emerge (or re-emerge) from the interfaces between animals and humans and the ecosystems in which they live'.[139] Following on, the FAO, World Organization for Animal Health (OIE), and World Health Organisation (WHO), published *A Tripartite Concept Note*, to 'develop normative standards and field programs to achieve One Health goals'.[140]

Meanwhile, the American Veterinary Medical Association pulled one health in another direction towards *A New Professional Imperative*, describing the 'concept of One Health [as] very much a strategy with a long-overdue bias towards health promotion and disease prevention across the human, animal, and environmental domains'.[141] And in 2019, the Climate and Environmental Foreign Policy Division at the German Federal Foreign Office and the WCS convened the *One Planet, One Health, One Future* conference to revisit the Manhattan Principles: their 'Call to Action' was organized about *The Berlin Principles on One Health*.[142] Their imperative was called 'joined-up ethical thinking' and used *solidarity* and *environmental justice* to anchor their reasons for returning to interspecific values.[143]

Then, in 2022, the WHO One Health High-Level Expert Panel (OHHLEP) defined one health as perhaps the first truly global health–environmental movement. In their operative definition, they called one health 'an integrated, unifying approach that aims to sustainably balance and optimize the health of people, animals and ecosystems', adding that '[one health] recognizes the health of humans, domestic and wild animals, plants, and the wider environment (including ecosystems) are closely linked and inter-dependent'. If this was nothing particularly new, then they added a new social imperative supporting social determinants of health:

> 'The approach mobilizes multiple sectors, disciplines and communities at varying levels of society to work together to foster well-being and tackle threats to health and ecosystems, while addressing the collective need for clean water, energy and air, safe and nutritious food, taking action on climate change, and contributing to sustainable development.'[144]

OHHLEP's definition was endorsed by the now *Quadripartite* consisting of the FAO, the United Nations Environment Programme (UNEP), WHO, and the World Organisation for Animal Health (now anglicized to WOAH). This bookend to the modern period of one health history perhaps represents a culmination of the tension between social and interspecific, even biocentric values. But, as we shall see, the mishmash of a social determinant of health framework with conservation and ecology remains a fragile compromise.

7.3 Different Histories

What can be concluded about the trajectory of one health over the years? Popularly, it is told through a selection of dividing chronological markers. Others likely see the value of the organic development of an approach that never took an explicit ethical turn: one health is just an evolving lens for addressing human health where there is contact at the animal–plant–environment interface. For many pioneers, however, the 'disease' was paramount and transformative of culture: for them, the natural animal was an object; its interests were entirely absent. When Calvin Schwabe spoke of veterinary public health, he alluded to a moral connection to animals only in the unique world of transhumant pastoralist cultures, and offered little by way of critique of the diverse history of animal ethics: he thought that Western veterinary public health could 'piggyback' offering *both* veterinary care and medicine when 'the welfare of their cattle represents the highest priority desire among these pastoral peoples'.[145]

The opportunity to explore a philosophical one health is all but absent from this history. Yet you can still find the influence of a philosophical egalitarianism or other social justifications for one health in practice.[146] Even so, there is an assumption that it is beyond question that (in the history of Western ideas) there is a long-standing 'great divide' between culture and nature. The argument goes like this: the fracture occurred during The Enlightenment, a period 'decisive in the making of [Western] modernity',[147] and grew through a series of technologies driving significant social change in industrialized and colonial worlds. The philosophies of this period are still held to be relevant in the critique of the Modern period: in their simplest, unanalysed forms, they continue to come up as 'the first' texts critical of the world *now as if it is* divided. But for historical accuracy, was a connecting theory really and entirely absent during all this? Bruno Latour writes: '. . . the problem is that almost *everyone* has messed up the definition of the West by taking it as its face value, taking up its own Master Narrative about having been modern; a narrative suggesting that the West was the place where a "scientific revolution" had occurred in such a way as to reveal the universal necessity of nature".[148]

The narrative that saw culture indomitably divided from nature is a pragmatic implication used to influence present social reflexivity – a kind of self-fulfilling prophecy to which we have grown accustomed, but a view that is static and weakly empirical. (To mention but a few, and though each would require its own Element volume to convey nuances,) René Descartes' (1596–1650) belief in 'animal automatism' is still used as the first proof of unnatural equality; but he thought it unlikely that animals were only machines, and, in fact, did not discount their feelings.[149] Thomas Hobbes' (1588–1679) social contract *did* exclude animals 'because not understanding our speech, they understand not, nor accept of any translation of right . . .',[150] but this was always a fictitious social contract that could materialize only as long as there are *natural persons* around.[151] For John Locke (1632–1704), 'personhood' [logically entailed from the colloquial use of 'man(kind)'] admitted of degrees so that, if animals "have any *Ideas* at all, and are not bare machines (as some would have them) we cannot deny them to have some reason";

> For were there a Monkey, or any Creature to be found, that had the use of Reason to such a degree, as to be able to understand general Signs, and to deduce Consequences about general *Ideas*, he would no doubt be subject to Law, and, in that Sense, be a *Man*, how much soever he differ'd in Shape from others of that Name.[152]

In David Hume's (1711–1776) naturalistic psychology, animals 'are endow'd with thought and reason as well as men'.[153] Immanuel Kant (1724–1804) argued

'So an understanding of man in terms of his species, as an earthy being endowed with reason, especially deserves to be called *knowledge of the world*, even though man is only one of the creatures of the world.'[154]

We are often told that Kant said we should avoid cruelty to animals *only* because it manifests in evil, and 'beings with wills' must perceive only the good of their deontological obligations. But even from this *logo*centric view, we might find fragments of rationality,[155] and that must mean the possibility of discovering wider-than-human agency. While Kant probably believed that non-human animals could not have wills, he did contemplate 'non-terrestrial rational beings'.[156]

And today's legal absurdities in animal rights can be traced back to Jeremy Bentham (1748–1832), who challenged 'ancient jurists' who class animals as 'things': 'The day may come, when the rest of the animal creation may acquire those rights which could never have been withholden from them but by the hand of tyranny.'[157]

John Stuart Mill (1806–1873) envisioned a universe 'secured to all mankind; and not to them only, but so far as the nature of things admits, to the whole sentient creation'.[158] He would be disappointed that still the law has not progressed.

In 1858, the most important connection between culture and nature of all was made: that humans were primates. And so, one health history must also wade through a time of controversies and tribulations faced by religious and scientific societies undergoing change. The anti-vivisection movement was growing then, too, led by religious groups, suffragettes, and literati advocating for the worth of animal lives (and admonishing their suffering) as part of the broad urgency for social reform. So, when Charles Darwin (1809–1882) showed what was possible from conceptual observations of Great Apes,[159] the utility of animal exploitation might have been questioned more, except many could not comprehend humans losing their apex status or becoming morally burdened (I wonder, is this still the case?).[160] Darwin wrote: 'He who understands baboon would do more towards metaphysics than Locke',[161] which at least suggested that some philosophers, like the evolutionists, were on the right track. The metaphysical doubt about humanity's uniqueness would eventually be vindicated by discoveries in genetic and neurological sciences insofar as there was now scientific proof.

An interesting waypoint of the time is Friedrich Engels' (1820–1895) critique of the ostracization of industrialized classes to unhealthy environments as 'social murder'.[162] As more faced the challenges of urbanization and industrialization, having left predominantly rural and agricultural life, the animals also went with them.

'For environmental historians, the rise of the environmental movement comes at the end of a story that begins before 1900. The first protests against pollution, the first efforts to conserve natural resources, and the first campaigns to save wilderness all occurred in the late nineteenth century.'[163]

Of course, no one knew the environmental catastrophes that had been set in motion with the British Industrial Revolution (1760 to 1840).[164] The 'anthropozoic' era had already started by 1883 (so-called by Antonio Stoppani, 1824–1891). Humans had for a long time been changing the land and therefore geological processes. Eduard Suess (1831–1914) first used the term *biosphere* in 1875, to refer to the surface that separates the planet (*geosphere*) from the cosmic medium; this is where you could find humans and all the other lifeforms. The *noösphere* (the 'thinking' or 'mind sphere') was coined sometime between Pierre Teilhard de Chardin (1881–1955), Édouard Le Roy (1870–1954), and Vladimir Vernadsky (1863–1945). The concept referred to an *in*scape (the essential inner nature of a person) that influences and affects the *land*scape; it was 'coextensive'[165] to the biosphere, a build-up of ideas, visible technologies, and impacts of development. Vernadsky noticed that in these respects, humanity was now a geological force transforming the planet.[166] He also saw the noösphere as an imperative to develop a commonwealth of scientific knowledge, thus predating global environmental problems and eventual international responses (which is considered in the second theme, Section 8). But for Vernadsky, anthropogenic change could be in *the interests of humanity*: if we were transitioning *to* the noösphere, then, teleologically speaking, perhaps we were escaping the biosphere altogether.

And so, perhaps there is a 'modern' prophetic point: humans have always been in the business of changing our environments. Perhaps not uniquely, but more than all other creatures, we find ourselves 'in' different environments; we are, as a species, nothing but adaptable because we are thinking. This undoubtedly coproduced unethical depletion of ecoservices, often along similar socialized lines observed by Engels. It is therefore quite natural to link one health to the 'beginning' of the Anthropocene Epoch. And maybe that is why zoonotic spillovers are *our* problem: on the one hand, I cannot help but think of the choices we make that contribute to pandemic risks; but on the other hand, pandemics stem from our indelible connections to nature. That tension suggests *we cannot escape* a natural state, and we are unlikely to avoid zoonoses as long as there is nature. But in this unfurnished (circular) idea, there is a prelude to our ethical responsibility to recognize that reality, as that relates to the chances of surviving the next pandemic.

7.4 Beginning an Ecological Era

It is perhaps no surprise then, that the eighteenth century is where the germinal 'one health' starts. How that it interpreted is up to the present reader. However, during this period, people were popularly starting to think about *their* rights and the rights of *others*. And the fact that contemporary Enlightenment thinkers were addressing similar issues is evidence that concern over environmentalism was in the air: it is an interlocking history of humanity's '... place in nature and human nature'.[167] There is much more that philosophers have done to explain the 'age-old connection' between '... landscapes, animal husbandry, forest, water, irrigation, about building cities, the circulation of air, the management of disease ....'.[168]

One health has a lexicon: 'links', 'relationships', 'holistic', 'interconnections', 'globalization', 'multi/inter/trans/another-disciplinarity'. But that list is also just a partial vocabulary of an idea moving forward (in a particular) social time. One health history could but does not include any number of environmental philosophies (some are mentioned later). And so, the popular story largely omits the tension between 'ethical' and 'in practice'; it is, for example, uncritical of the dissection, drugging, and inoculations of animals. A little digging, in far from obscure works, tells us much more about humanity's relationship with the universe. If the alternative *is* also the story of one health, then it began in a time in which *human* rights were discovered, and new thinking emerged to challenge the parochial values of medicine, economics, industry, and law.

Drawing this theme to a close, then, is not so much because it is a dead end; there is a great deal more travel in the history of philosophy. In the one health story, philosophers have been mostly left alone to critique the great divide from their lofty ivory towers. Engaging with this in finite detail will reveal their contributions to global ethical thinking.

8 Theme Two: One Health and Human Rights

Environmentalism in the United Nations (UN) is defined as the *Human Right to a Clean, Healthy and Sustainable Environment*[169]:

> 'Human flourishing is not possible without a biodiverse, life-sustaining Earth system. This is recognized in the United Nations' 17 Sustainable Development Goals.'[170]

So, in this theme, I assume *prima facie* that human rights frame international law. My criticism is that *human* rights augment existing structures that bring public health into conflict with conservation, because they are also concepts that must differentiate human beings (all of them?) from (all) non-human animals.

I'll attempt to reconcile that tension (ultimately unsuccessfully) over the next few pages. The present thematic question, therefore, is how a *universal* concept of one health is for every*one*, everywhere?

Recognizing that international law is a contentious area of political intrigue, academic theorizing, and judicial revision, rights talk may have a certain familiar ring but one that may not always be consistent. I am not going to provide a comprehensive legalese definition of international law.[171] Principally, my aim in this theme is to establish the fact that the international laws concerning the environment consist of the essential features of 'human dignity, human rights and fundamental freedoms'.[172] Human rights belong to human beings simply because they are human beings regardless of whether they are recognized as legal persons in a particular jurisdiction: ' ... all human rights are universal, indivisible, interdependent and interrelated'.[173] As part of the international legal system, rights seem to be part of the furniture of the world. Again, my purpose is not to devalue human rights – in and of themselves, the precarious status of rights around the world attest to their importance.

My anchor point is the UN's *Universal Declaration of Human Rights* (UDHR). The Declaration is said to be rooted in Western politics;[174] yet there are many sources that bridge national identity to international law, such as regional communities like the African Union's Charter (1986), Arab Charter on Human Rights (2004), Council of Europe (1949), and the Inter-American Commission on Human Rights (1959). Which is to say that philosophically human rights have a commonality: human dignity, ' ... the infrastructure on which the modern superstructure of human rights is constructed'.[175] In this respect, John Baragahare writes:

> ... Moral ideas, theories and principles, whether from Africa, West, or the East are prima facie applicable in so far as they are proportionately and significantly integrative in the resolution of a specific morally problematic situation in Africa.
>
> ... we further need to bear in mind the liberal human rights tradition that is already deeply entrenched in most African public institutions and deeply internalized by Africans.[176]

And similarly, Eduardo Gudynas describes the features of the concept of *Buen Vivir* across South America as a 'harmonious relationship between "society" and "nature"'.[177] He adds,

> 'Some Western ideas, particularly those related to critiques of Modernity, were included in Buen Vivir. The concept of Nature's rights, in the sense of a recognition of intrinsic values in nonhuman beings, stemmed from Western environmental discourses, which were then "mixed" (articulated, fused, etc.) ....'[178]

Amartya Sen, in 1997, asserted the universalism of human rights: 'The case for liberty and political rights turns ultimately on their basic importance and on their instrumental role. This case is as strong in Asia as it is elsewhere.'[179] He was making a political critique of cultural exceptionalism in a world with porous borders, visible democratic deficits, and countries with long and complex histories.

So it should go without saying that even a commonality of human rights might create conflicts in one health funding, priorities, and ideologies. But what we're interested in are conflicts apparent between human rights and animal welfare.[180] Such dichotomies were explored in the first theme as culture and nature; that is a remarkably similar division in respect to a political theory of human rights and a biological rendering of the rights of *all* human beings. It is hard to escape the sense that, if international law is taken on face value, then *any legal* approach to one health is anthropocentric. But legal judgements are clearly moral, too: they are 'major issues of political philosophy with significant ramifications for the lives of many people';[181] and, as Deryck Beyleveld and Roger Brownsword argue, morality is necessarily connected to legality.[182] A moral question we must answer, then, is whether rights are really *human* rights? Taking this cue, then, we should ask whether a one health approach, based in international law, can ever achieve a natural form of interspecies justice?

8.1 Legal Approaches in International Law

George Annas argues that the UDHR 'itself sets forth the ethics of public health ...'.[183] According to this account, one health is already embedded in green issues conceptualized as *social justice*; that, as we shall see in theme three, frames most if not all common ethical discourse. So, arguably, organizations endorsing one health within the UN's auspices, are guided by (if not bound to) the core goal to secure human rights, too. This would apply to the *Quadripartite* of the FAO, UNEP, WHO, and WOAH.

This much is clear in the transformation of the UDHR into treaty form through the *International Covenant on Civil and Political Rights* and the *International Covenant on Economic Social and Cultural Rights* (1966): these are rights only human beings have, and they are conditional on protecting the environment in areas like trade, food security, and humanitarianism.[184] *The UN Paris Climate Agreement* (2015) explicitly acknowledges that:

> '... when taking action to address climate change, [Parties must] respect, promote and consider their respective obligations on human rights, the right to health, the rights of indigenous peoples, local communities, migrants,

children, persons with disabilities and people in vulnerable situations and the right to development, as well as gender equality, empowerment of women and intergenerational equity'.

And the UN's Educational, Scientific and Cultural Organization's (UNESCO) *Universal Declaration on Bioethics and Human Rights* (2005) states:

> Aware that human beings are an integral part of the biosphere, with an important role in protecting one another and other forms of life, in particular animals, . . .
>
> [and] . . . to underline the importance of biodiversity and its conservation as a common concern of humankind [Article 2(h))].
>
> Due regard is to be given to the interconnection between human beings and other forms of life . . . [Article 17].

But animals do not have (human) rights; that is not what due regard means.[185] Even the UN *Kunming-Montreal Global Biodiversity Framework* (2022), which is remarkable by affirming [where they are recognized] the ' . . . rights of nature and rights of Mother Earth, [are] an integral part of its successful implementation', (p. 5) – and even namedropping the 'One Health Approach' (Section C(r)) – states that, ultimately,

> 'The implementation of the framework should follow a human rights-based approach, respecting, protecting, promoting and fulfilling human rights' (p. 6).[186]

But there *is* something different: the UN's Environment Programme's (UNEP) *Convention on Biological Diversity* (CBD, 1993) (under which the *Kunming Framework* was created). Here, Article 22.1 states:

> 'The provisions of this Convention shall not affect the rights and obligations of any contracting Party deriving from any existing international agreement, *except where the exercise of those rights and obligations would cause a serious damage or threat to biological diversity*' (my emphasis).

Is this a form of interspecies law? An unusual measure, perhaps, where conservation can be legitimately weighed against the public interest? That is a remote chance: the opportunities for interspecific rights in international law are few, especially in the contexts where animals might seek protection from humans.[187] Consider the following examples:

1. The exception clause in the CBD (Article 22,) is meant to create compatibility with older conventions subject to customary international law; few relevant laws exist, but perhaps the *International Whaling Convention* (1946), *Convention on International Trade in Endangered Species of Wild Fauna and Flora* (CITES) (1975), or the UN's *Convention on the Law of the Sea* (1994)

might create grounds for appeals to protect certain animals? These are far from expressions of fundamental *animal rights*; and I am not aware that the CBD has been tested in court in respect to what 'serious damage or threat' means to biodiversity and where the threshold is met which would limit human rights.[188] The protection of biological diversity relates to 'Biological resources' – these are 'genetic resources, organisms or parts thereof, populations, or any other biotic component of ecosystems with actual or potential use or value for humanity'.[189] Beyond past law, the UN *Agreement Under the United Nations Convention on the Law of the Sea on the Conservation and Sustainable Use of Marine Biological Diversity of Areas Beyond National Jurisdiction* (2023), Article 7, requires an 'ecosystem approach'.[190] But there are no rights arising out of this otherwise transformative agreement. Instead, all that means is that the 'objectives of management of land, water and living resources are a matter of societal choice. . . . [but] Ecosystems should be managed for their intrinsic values and for the tangible or intangible benefits for humans, in a fair and equitable way'.[191] The first clause indicates a tension that we'll return to, yet it is abundantly clear that this new agreement creates no *intrinsic* animal rights. So humanitarian collisions with nature are mostly avoided because animals are not subjects in the same way to human law.

2. The law remains uncertain about the difference between factual and fictional rights, and often as a consequence provides contradictions about moral persons and legal persons.[192] For example, Cheryl Macpherson suggests that some wanted the ' . . . scope of the [UNESCO's *Universal Declaration on Bioethics and Human Rights*] . . . to encompass all life forms, not just human life', but the final draft was worded 'vaguely enough to be interpreted to everyone's satisfaction'.[193]

   There is, it turns out, little satisfaction for animals. A recent decision in the Court of Appeals of New York in the United States confirmed what amounts to quite entrenched reasoning, by deciding that an elephant (*Elephas maximus*) called Happy, who was confined to the Bronx Zoo, had no legal rights.[194] It is hard not to see this as anything but an inevitable outcome, because the relevant law only concerns the social, economic, and cultural rights that appeal to the public interest. Although the Judges in the majority recognized what Happy *was* – elephants have naturally social and cultural lives – the law must protect society against the 'enormous destabilizing impacts' and 'perilous implications' of giving animals like *this* elephant equal status to humans.[195]

   As far as this thematic analysis is plausible, principles like those of the WHO's OHHLEP are interpretable within the framework of rights, too; so that is how we must interpret their *One Health Theory of Change*.[196] The first principle – 'Equity between sectors and disciplines' – might be used to exclude those that disproportionately contribute to climate change or damage ecosystems through excessive extraction (see Example 4). The second principle calls for 'Sociopolitical and multicultural parity (the doctrine that all people are equal and deserve equal rights and opportunities) . . .', except there is no reading of the relationship between principles one and two: can we say that bad actors forfeit their chances of equity? But then there is 'principle three:

'Socioecological equilibrium that seeks a harmonious balance between human–animal–environment interaction and acknowledging the importance of biodiversity, access to sufficient natural space and resources, and the intrinsic value of all living things within the ecosystem.'

This might very well contradict principle two: how do we use humanitarianism of human rights to come to terms with the biocentrism of valuing *all living things*?

3. Persistent environmental degradation undermined many of the WHO's Millennium Development Goals that were supposed to be achieved by 2015.[197] A weakness was 'a symbolic, rather than systematic treatment of the environment in the goals',[198] which suggested that ' . . . key aspects of the environment must be clearly represented in the broader post-2015 agenda'.[199] Arguably, all of the SDGs relate in one way or another to 'the environment', but specific goals on 'climate action' (SDG13), 'life below water' (SDG14), and 'life above ground' (SDG15) address unsustainable ecoservices causal to the displacement of people. But there is a risk that many of the SDGs will not be met by the close of 2030 either.[200] The International Council for Science concluded 'that the [SDG] framework as a whole might not be internally consistent – and as a result not be sustainable'.[201] Viktoria Spaiser et al. 'quantified this inconsistency and showed that economic growth fulfils socioeconomic goals while simultaneously hindering environmental goals'.[202] This tension can be a broader philosophical point: ' . . . achieving those [SDGs] requires that human societies exercise self-aware self-regulation. Yet, maintaining a self-regulating, human life–supporting planet is not the primary goal of some dominant modes of collective human activity today'.[203]

4. The Quadripartite's *One Health Joint Plan of Action* (2022) calls for enhancing 'private-sector' engagement[204] on the condition that they are 'measurably contributing to halting the degradation of the environment and to promoting its conservation and restoration'.[205] Certain industries are responsible for a larger part of environmental public bads. In many instances, they have been involved in patchy ethical behaviour under the influence of politics[206] and 'green washing'[207] – from still being the sources of environmental pollution, to leading in the capture of public goods.[208] If we have reasons *in principle* to exclude such groups (as part of a *One Health Theory of Change*), then how do

we understand similar co-benefits, risks, trade-offs, and opportunities of 'conservation that are conflictual with public health?'[209]

That is, if 'Public health is a public good, wildlife is a common-pool resource in most parts of the world, and zoonoses are a negative externality that can stem from the wildlife trade for human consumption, compromising public health and, in turn, economic activity.'[210]

One health is already vulnerable to the ideas of neoclassical economists: for example, deep environmental philosophy (a 'cuss word' among economists),[211] is neither 'pragmatic' (a seamless web in which there is coherence among beliefs) nor 'urgent and eminently practical'.[212] Economists will tell us that markets, after all, are *self-evidently* a human good, even a positive economic determinant of health.[213] But the capitalist business class's environmental concerns – their *social capital*[214] – are guided by ethics likely to be self-serving and of self-preservation (I am generalizing here; but will let the record speak for itself). It is hard to see how the sacrosanct premise that 'goods'[215] are tradable can contribute to a debate about nature's inherent moral value.[216]

Perhaps, instead, a 'one health economy' is merely a subset of the natural ecosystem which allows us to better see its socialistic flaws.[217] These are reasons for including perspectives that *will* lead to the end of exploitative activities, to include incentives for ethical rewilding and ecological restoration, and to commit to purposes that are harmonious with nature. But we must be willing to change dogma and therefore the face of laws: compare, for instance, how a tree with legal standing or river with rights (a 'radical new theory or myth' spreading around the world),[218] can be stripped of meaning as lumber or bottled water. (And to compare that to how corporations have *become* protected 'legal entities' or personalities.)

In pointing out the limits of international law, that is not to say that there are no opportunities: the point is to connect the thread from human rights to theoretical indeterminateness about legal status, biological resources, and the flow of goods between social-ecological systems.

If one health ethics is about challenging unfairness and resisting unreasonable capture of ecoservices, it could do better by resisting the ' ... triumph of capitalism – which had closed any debate about the type of society and economic system we might want and refocused the debate on how to manage the only system we have'.[219] International law is deeply connected to ecosystem health[220] and human well-being,[221] but it also linked to the problems of environmental capture and corruption. My remedy in this respect is simple: we need to be clear about the cards we have (and critical of why and how they were dealt), and to question what we want the common or public good to mean, and, if necessary, with the aid of philosophical enquiry.

8.2 A New Rights Organization

John Rawls writes, 'Justice is the first virtue of social institutions, as truth is of systems of thought. A theory however elegant and economical must be rejected or revised if it is untrue; likewise, laws and institutions no matter how efficient and well-arranged must be reformed or abolished if they are unjust.'[222]

Rawls' 'decent system of social cooperation' entails that animals are not entitled to justice – only compassion – because they are, in the traditional Kantian sense, neither moral nor legal persons. Bruno Latour also contends that ' . . . the parliament in which a common world could be assembled has got to be constructed from scratch'.[223] For Latour, the global identity of climate change can only be made sense of as a 'cosmopolitics' – the plurality of the *common world* must be harmonious. What might that governance look like? Well, he imagines a potentially new 'political ecology' – '*What term other than ecology would allow us to welcome nonhumans into politics?*' –[224] and a 'Parliament of Things' representing the interests of humans, non-human organisms, systems, and objects:[225] '[citing Amita Baviskar] What counts is not if you are religious or secular, but if you manage to protect *humans* from being defined without the cosmos that provide their life support, and *nature* from being understood without humans that have collaborated with non-humans for eons.'[226]

If I may be permitted, I can make this into a practical argument. Imagine an insect. This insect is a member of a species that has been responsible for millions of human deaths; and its only discernible purpose is to spread illnesses to and between humans. We cannot hold this insect personally responsible, as it has no rights and neither does the plasmodium it harbours. (Though Latour might say that both have agency – they are visible, thinkable, representable – a mix or hybrid of culture and nature). We can spray a pesticide that kills the insect or severely depletes its population; other genetic technologies could wipe out the species.[227] In this imaginary case, if the extirpation of the vector is plausible, then we can likely shrink the burden of disease for impacted communities: the act, it seems, is demanded by public health. But let us also say that the pesticide indiscriminately kills *all* insects (or transposons allow the gene modifications to spread between species). From an ecological perspective, this becomes a disaster: insects are pollinators and food for other animals. As a result of human action, flowers cannot reproduce, and animals are poisoned by the pesticide leaching into ground water. Eventually, the pesticide will build up in rivers and lakes and will affect human health. That final social harm stemmed from a tiny insect with (only in our minds) a remote connection to us. Can we connect the life of such an insect to human rights?

Of course, this methodological analysis is not imaginary. It might be true that no one would particularly miss the mosquito, except perhaps for the western mosquitofish (*Gambusia affinis*). But in 1962, Rachel Carson published *Silent Spring*, calling attention to the environmental effects of indiscriminate use of the pesticide dichlorodiphenyltrichloroethane (DDT).[228] She acknowledged that, on the one hand, the burden of community malaria justifies effective insect vector control (which involves several evidence-based approaches such as antimalarial medication, insecticide-treated nets, and indoor residual spraying). But, on the other hand, DDT is not only indiscriminate, but is also a carcinogen, and its metabolites are persistent in the environment and a long-term source of exposure. It is now *also* acknowledged that DDT is toxic to wildlife. Is there a balance? As a result of DDT being banned in some places in the 1970s, critics drew a direct line from *Silent Spring* to the failure to eradicate malaria in developing countries. In fact, Carson's narrative was not ignorant to the blight of mosquitoes on communities, and she advocated for responsible use of technologies to avoid long-term human health problems (which would include environmental protection).

One health might take practical inspiration from *Silent Spring* but for the persistent question of what ethically counts. Now we seem to be covering the same ground again: bees (clade *Anthophila*) are vulnerable to neonicotinoids, and these insecticides are banned in some places, but their use is controversial and dynamic due to political indecision and industry influence. Bee species are essential pollinators around the world and are in sharp decline everywhere due to cumulative stressors.[229] They face many factors causing their populations to collapse, to the extent that it is beyond reasonable doubt that without an environmental response of some kind, the bees' downfall will also be ours.[230]

This has a cascading effect that eventually activates public health responses; bees are dying around the world, effecting industrial and local farmers. There is no simple solution: agrochemicals are a powerful lobby group, and the SDGs potentially require intensive chemical farming that is economically defensible. Approaches to bee health (especially honeybees, *Apis mellifera*) include antibiotic use – which potentially adds to the global crisis in antimicrobial resistance. Antibacterial overuse is often interpreted differently as a clinical, veterinary, and agricultural problem (but they are indelibly linked). And now bee health is also a bioethical issue: gene editing is being considered to create enhanced 'Frankenbees'.[231] Once the mosquito is poisoned or engineered out of existence, we might go further … (or make a mistake).[232] And if we just make such choices referring to public health as *the* public interest, then someone might think it is a much safer world with no bats (so no COVID). Or no nature.

And so, we are back at the narrative of *An(other) Environmental Crisis* from the start of this Element: does one health ethics reveal all the key players' ethics, ideologies, and politics? A microbiologist (or biologist, conservationist, ecologist, entomologist, ethologist, zoologist, etc.) might tell you their interests signify a '. . . focus on the interlinking of human and animal realms (and indeed the realms of microorganisms, insects and so forth) . . . quite distinct from an approach that sees contact with animals as a set of interactions that primarily create risk to humans'.[233]

Where are the human rights? Perhaps they are only part of one health: an awareness of a human noöspheric zeitgeist allows us to go beyond comparative medicine and veterinary presence, towards environmentalism – a version of justice that registers impacts beyond the carefully crafted public health norms made by the supposedly conflict-free groups at the tables of the WHO and UN.

But a *science of the biosphere* tells us much more; and if the great task ahead suggests this positive legal theme is a dead end, that certainly does not mean that awareness of one health has no role on the international level. Urgency (and *realpolitik*) perhaps requires us to turn a blind eye to too-complex interests when in global courts, and we commit to a priority for 'social welfare'; a worthy ambition no doubt, but one that excludes nature for the sake of a risky technological 'revolution'. We should at least keep a close eye on how such arguments are used to obscure other possible goals, and injure the natural and 'social environment'.[234]

9 Theme Three: One Health Ethics

I started this Element in New York, where a group of experts met under a banner of one health to unify conservation and global health. We tracked that story in theme one, towards a fully fledged definition of one health that *implied* a version of biocentrism. In theme two, I suggested that a 'new' forum for one health would be necessary because the scope of international law does not recognise animal rights. So far, then, the assumption persists that one health is public health. And that in-and-of-itself tells us who one health is for. But it is important that we avoid positivism in this regard: it is not enough just to say that human rights exist in international law so that's how we must frame one health. I have taken these first two themes as far as I can here. In the third theme, I ask, does bioethics take us further in our analysis of whom is a theory of one health *for*?

Instead of trying to extend human rights (as the saying goes, it is rather like 'squeezing blood from a turnip'), we could revisit first principles – 'rights talk' extends to our non-human companions, and it has consequences visible in the soil and air that impact on beings we have never met (or perhaps cannot know), living far from the places decisions are made, and likely to suffer after our agreements are concluded. In a few words, one health is a theory of *ecological environmentalism* – it is uniquely a theory of interspecific justice, a 'one-ness' of health between the species. So I explore this idea next: one health does not just describe environments – these were already visible through the anthropocentric lens of public health – but connects our mutual moral well-being to nature.

9.1 Philosophy

Steven Jay Gould might have said that I am claiming that one health has an 'essence'. There is a test to pass: the 'conclusions are the consequence, not the essence ... Avoidance of nuclear war is fundamentally an ethical and political imperative, but we must know the factual consequences to make firm judgments'.[235] Does one health have an ethical imperative? My answer would be something like: 'Environmentalism is ethically more than preventing an unsightly vista or cleaning up a rotten environment; environmental protection should not be seen as an inconvenience or an economic cost: nature's collapse is the end of humanity. And so, we know more than the consequences.'

But, when we get down to the weeds, that means there are going to be complex obligations (or duties), for example, ' ... to preserve antimicrobial efficacy and ensure *sustainable and equitable access* to antimicrobials for responsible and prudent use *in human, animal and plant health*'; or to 'Protect and restore biodiversity, prevent the degradation of ecosystems and the wider environment to *jointly support* the health of people, animals, plants and ecosystems, underpinning sustainable development' (my emphasis).[236] 'Sustainable', 'equitable', and 'jointly' are ethically weighty concepts (just like dignity, upon which human rights cling to), so do these right actions really extend to animals? Will animals have *prudent* access to medications? And will *burdens* be placed on human communities as a result?

These obligations come in many forms. In theme one, we saw how nature was always a philosophical puzzle outside of the mainstream one health narrative (and it has been disappointing that little has been made of this). These connections have been an important anchor in environmental philosophy. For example: Albert Schweitzer (1875–1965) called them *Reverence for Life*.[237] Aldo Leopold (1887–1948) thought that an organism's well-being was 'a matter of biotic right': a 'thing is right', he wrote, 'when it tends to preserve the integrity, stability, and beauty of the biotic community. It is wrong when it tends otherwise'.[238] Arne Naess (1912–2009) argued for *Biospherical Egalitarianism*.[239] Mary Anne Warren (1946–2010) believed that animal rights and environmentalism are different but complementary matters: animals also stand to benefit or suffer from human actions.[240] Paul W. Taylor (1923–2015) split human rights from *Respect for Nature*.[241] Tom Regan (1938–2017) thought all animals were *Subjects of a Life*.[242] Mary Midgley (1919–2018) said there was a mixed community: 'We are not just rather like animals; we are animals'.[243] And Holmes Rolston III (1932–) penned: 'Remove eagles from the sky and we will suffer a spiritual loss'.[244] I am not going to take any of these theories further, because we know that practically speaking, there will be many more ideas (and interests) that appeal to each of us; in the end, together we simply do not *know* how to treat animals.

We *know* we are heading towards environmental catastrophe, as any[245] environmental scientist will tell you; and wherever we end up, even if we have to flee this rock, the choices will tell a story of the indelible essence of human survival (history) and prosperity (economics) and nature's resilience (conservation), our grasp on justice (ethics) and acts of exploitation (social sciences), our responsibility and guilt (philosophy), or perhaps, our ultimate demise (the end?). Thus, disciplines that once focussed on understanding discrete systems are now about understanding change in ecological-social systems *and reasons* to safeguard wildlife and habitats. One health is as much about the normativity of 'our' rights and duties towards those we share the planet with, questioning the self-serving 'wisdom' of economies, and ultimately reacting to (un)fair environmental policies.

So philosophers on a global stage must be part of the answer. In cannon, little has been said about the *practical* circumstances of a human world connected to nature. Even less has been done in respect to the questions philosophers have grappled with for eons: what is essential about who 'we' are and what we are related to; these natural questions need interdisciplinary study. (And if these questions seem rather abstract, they have in fact been addressed many times to understand public health.) The environmental movements of the mid-twentieth century were a response to human influence as a dominant (but not always welcome) force in the known universe. As we gained a scientific understanding of whole systems – a *science of the biosphere* – conservationists, ecologists, and environmentalists started to talk about the causes, trajectories, and impacts of *social* change. In the Anthropocene, it was said, 'moral choices will be essential'.[246] That speaks to human efforts to improve the environment rather than merely accepting to live with it, and perhaps that ship has sailed anyway, because *to do nothing* now would be to absolve our responsibility. But we can question the poor choices made so far, especially those intended to capitalize nature by exploitation, capture, and consumption.

9.2 Frames of Ethics

The lack of theoretical work in one health cannon has not been cost neutral. Pursuing multiple 'one health' approaches in an uncoordinated fashion – a cynical criticism of environmentalism, but perhaps one with elements of truth[247] – creates fallacious duties and unanticipated consequences. Disagreements about the environment have become relative problems: 'Economic policymakers have concentrated on growth, developmentalists on the distribution of the benefits of growth, and conservationists on the costs and consequences of growth for nature and the environment.'[248] One health has advocates who ' ... constantly seek to secure their own resources, establish their legitimacy, deploy technical scientific and technological experts and craft global responses and norms'.[249] As a result, there are concerns that the movement is becoming 'splintered', as key groups are ' ... competing for attention and funding for their programmatic priorities'.[250] 'Dominant sectors and stakeholders, typically from the human and public health community, can affect the One Health agenda and direct resources and political and financial attention to issues they perceive to be a priority.'[251]

The predictable dynamics between funding and policy tend to reach an uneasy equilibrium; they claim one health 'speaks' to their values despite having potentially discrete intentions.

Fractures appear in academia – a group responsible for authenticating the progress of one health – as some look to the edges of their own subjects for ethical inspiration; but here they cannot always find qualitative evidence to support the imaginative and possible futures they envisage. Voices are being excluded; some of these we might not want to hear because they are 'harmfully formed groups',[252] but, in all but the most extreme cases, there are few objective criteria to justify their ostracization (in one example, 'so-called experts' only speak to a narrow agenda that ultimately serves populist strategies). Sparring between disparate groups increases noise and contradictions, and allows destructive opinions to control the political debate.

The environmental debate needs help. Philosophers could oblige, but they are rarely seen in public supporting the one health movement. Perhaps there is a suspicion that one health ethics might not stand apart from other concepts,[253] or that such efforts are unnecessary (the benefits of one health are self-evident), or that the demand for logical rigour may undermine practice.[254] Philosophy can start with the definitions: we get practically nowhere if one health 'could mean whatever people want [it] to'.[255] Responses like these create 'catchy and appropriate' slogans;[256] meanings are lost or become blurry. And if one health is not meant to be defined, then we merely hitch the horses to an uncritical ideology. The one health approach becomes nothing new; we are stuck in a circle of assumptions about impossible outcomes; and, as a perspective policy framework, one health lacks guts. The causes for concern (and disappointment in the progress of the approach) become a demand for 'more *insert discipline here* work is needed' but it is rarely done.

Until then, the movement borrows from existing health principles: 'Public health ethics sees the health of population groups and communities as central to public policies that mediate individual and collective actions by promoting conditions that sustain human flourishing. Public health ethics arguments can support and justify the types of sustainable collective action on which the success of a One Health approach depends.'[257]

Yet the field ends up as divided as the two faces of modern bioethics.[258] Bioethics has a distinct origin. Fritz Jahr argued 'Bio-ethiks' was a 'Categorical Imperative' (an *a posteriori* or imperfect duty) to 'Regard every living being in principle as an end in itself and treat it accordingly as far as possible'; his 'approach was to bridge the gap between ethics and science . . . [and] blurred the boundaries between human and animal suffering'.[259] Van Rensselaer Potter's 'Global Bioethics' was inspired by the Leopold's Land Ethic, 'a long-term view that is concerned with what we must do to preserve the ecosystem in a form that is compatible with the continued existence of the human species'.[260] But *medical* ethics as it had become had little time for such ideas – it was absurd to say that *all* animals are equal,[261] or our interests lie with buzzing insects,[262] *for þæm þe* 'Ye are of more value than many sparrows'.[263] Even 'A *summum boium* of preserving trees has no place in an ethic of social justice.'[264]

One health ethics is therefore a necessary enquiry to prevent the emergent field from compounding such contradicting values. We already find seeming irreconcilable dichotomies; to the great divide, we can now add local/global and private/public. There should be a sense in which, for one health, ethical pluralism is not just pragmatic; the risks of irreparable disagreement are too high to allow 'professional discretion' or 'scientific controversy' to decide matters. In the final analysis, different practices of culling, vaccination, or other response to zoonoses, are (un)professional, (un)scientific, or (un)ethical according to the formation of certain professional, practical, and normative views.

9.3 Two Kinds of Environmentalism

The metaphor of *ethical frames* is meant to help us see all the possible subjects, views, and interpretations of a topic. But if we are choosing a frame, there are many shades, technicalities, and discrepancies between them, and we need to decide which to hang on the parliament's walls and in judicial chambers. It should be clear by now that in one health, we can imagine two kinds of environmentalisms resting on two kinds of theoretical assumptions; the problem, as we shall see, is how a *reasonable environmentalist* can make sense of these seemingly conflicting 'framework' ideologies.

Social environmentalism might have other names, such as population health or environmental public health. There are three factors: it concerns the conditions of health that are more often beyond the reach of individuals acting alone; health is influenced by the actions of others; and health is impacted by economic, legal, political, and social influences called the determinants of health. These determinants are causes of morbidity and mortality in populations and are key drivers of environmental harms; these include population stratifications along many axes,[265] such that the '[c]ritical needs of [persons] today, in addition to the combatting of his diseases and for enough food, [includes] adequate environmental quality, and a society in which humane values prevail'.[266]

Likewise, economic and legal determinants of health follow an experiential gradient with respect to the conditions under which persons are born, grow, live, work, and age. Environmentalism therefore concerns green issues that define ' . . . a set of cultural and political responses to a crisis in humans' relationships with their surroundings',[267] and directly relates to concepts of community and kinship, and the bonds they have between generations.[268] As a result, one health focusses on inequality between groups, to develop a broad range of perspectives about 'who benefits' (e.g., from a green economy) and 'who bears the burdens' (e.g., of pollution). Ultimately, the ' . . . population the [public health] approach speaks to includes all born, living human beings within the jurisdiction of a Liberal State . . . and denies a *special* normative protection to potential members that some theorists would *in*clude' [citing Peter Singer's *Animal Liberation*].[269]

As Baird Callicott writes, even Darwin thought the 'boundaries of the moral community [were] coextensive with the boundaries of the perceived social community. And sentient beings, so far as Darwin knew, did not form a community with man [sic]'.[270] Applying social justice as a frame, therefore, might include 'everyone who should be "in"',[271] and that in and of itself is discerning of the 'human good' of an ecosystem.[272] It appeals to those with an anthropocentric view.

But some cultures place humans and animals *in the same communities*.[273] Such *ecological environmentalism* is a constellation of views, that, among other things, confronts the anthropocentric's claim that nature's value is contingent on human interests, and suggests that view might even put the environment – and therefore humans – at risk. *Ecological justice* reflects on the conditions for conserving sustainable resources that such communities need to flourish.

Therefore, it is not enough to call something 'one health' just because it concerns 'the environment'. Public health involves 'the environment' as a space for *social* justice. For example, the scourge of tobacco-related illness also relates to the environmental determinants of health, such as passive exposure and the regulation of tobacco farming. One health, however, has connotations to *ecological* justice – the destruction of wilderness to make way for tobacco cultivation requires a lens to reconcile conservation (the interests of threatened animals and environments), health (the impact of extensive regional burning to clear land), and economic growth (the privatization of natural resources). But I also think we must be careful not to see these environmentalisms in opposition. The social environmentalist might justify excluding animals from moral considerations under public health: animals are at worst vectors, hosts, and reservoirs; they are vermin and expendable. They might see companionship and other connections to animals as subjectively believable, but violations of *human* rights are tangible. Conversely, ecological justice is compatible with public health because it does not exclude human beings. To make progress, we must move on from a narrative that one health is just public health, towards a contemporary theory to explain *both* as existing in the same *coextensive space*.

9.4 Procedural Ethics

This Element is not the last word on such a space. The point is not to find a finished thing: a United Nations-like institution with a fully formed social history and moral purpose (that was explored in theme two). I use coextensive in an informal sense. That word was used to superimpose the noösphere upon the biosphere. Similarly, as ethical predicates, one health and public health are close-knit and threaded together in a complex tapestry; they are occupying the same space and time but cannot be reduced to each other. I emphasize a space – which can be a conceptual argument, or an actual place – because being present and engaged in debate allows knowledge to emerge from where we find ourselves; how we disentangle the ideas in these places is a considerable challenge.

Environmentalists are part of much larger polycentric, or cultural ecosystems: these are the structural and normative institutions we create to make political decisions as 'experts', 'government', and 'publics'.[274] It is where we mingle with one another in institutions of law and economics, and seek representation from government, and the support from NGOs. Despite inevitable conflicts, there is a strong affinity to 'perfect' social-economic networks and solutions in the special circumstances or 'dramas' that communities face.[275] In philosophy, too, there is a vast literature to solve the problems of engagement between centres in pluralistic societies. A basic premise is that democracies create frameworks for debating 'ethics' as long as ethical participation is guaranteed. After that, debates are governed by the cocreation of clusters of norms,[276] or rules arising from likeminded values. We might then critically judge the quality of debate using fully formed concepts such as Jürgen Habermas' communities of 'Ideal Speech': one of his vital contributions is that choices made under ideal conditions are 'true'.[277] But that must be questionable: what this doesn't tell us about are the implied normative foundations existing prior to debate. For example, we might find that 'dignity' is in the fabric of communities of human rights, and so that a deliberative framework that is 'undignified' would always be unethical. Procedural ethics, for instance, defines engagement (or deliberative ethics) as ostensibly ethical only in jurisdictions wedded to civil and political rights; if such rights were merely subjective, then fair debate would be impossible.[278] In fact, practical discourse of any kind logically presupposes commitment to a moral form that includes no net costs to participation. But the fact that foundational premises are often left out often overburdens ideal speech to do all the ethical work. Consider this sequence:

'Whether the blue whale survives should not have to depend on what humans know or what they see on television. Human interests and preferences are far too parochial to provide a satisfactory basis for deciding on what is environmentally desirable.'[279]

It is 'extraordinary difficult to produce a "public" concerned with ecological problems because of the enormous complexity, the long distance between causes and consequences, the lag time, the rupture in scale, and the erasure of national and administrative boundaries'.[280]

The causes of climate change are 'controversial', despite 'greater than 99% consensus' in the peer-reviewed scientific literature that it is anthropogenic.[281] The evidence suggests that climate change increases the risks of pandemics.

'After much discussion, debate, and research, the Oxford Dictionaries Word of the Year 2016 is "post-truth"'—an adjective defined as 'relating to or denoting circumstances in which objective facts are less influential in shaping public opinion than appeals to emotion and personal belief.'

These conditions illustrate significant problems for framework approaches; neither 'side' emerges from an entirely unbiased culture base (and we might think that each is a 'check and balance' on the other).[282] Each ideology (or their causes) will bait the other to antagonise science/experts, publics/communities, private/industry, and policy/political. Each contains many unspoken 'ethical' concepts, too, that will pull at every facet of democratic decision making. (This is the problem, for example, of rightfully excluding 'harmfully informed groups', mentioned in Section 9.2, without first defining exactly what is harmful about their ideology.) In the end, everyone speaks to different ideas of inclusion, debatable topics, and ethical solutions, which form the *clusters* of fair-ish procedures, just (about) laws, socially engaged participants, and outcomes finely balanced on good faith.

I am sceptical that in all these views there is always 'common-sense',[283] or at least, a commonality that emerges from the platitudes of engagement. For every opponent of animal research or vivisection, there is a view lambasting the refusal 'to recognise the moral difference between species';[284] assuring us of the ' . . . true dependence – far greater than publicly understood – of continuing medical progress upon animal observations and experiments';[285] and that 'Given a little time, the petishist millions might, perhaps, take a good look at their beloved 'familiars' and admit that the evolutionary gap between them and us is too wide to bridge and that instead of trying to narrow it, they should attempt to make it wider.'[286]

I'll end this section with some observations to keep my case onside (although I believe too little is made of the facts just stated in explaining the fallibility of community engagement). The ideal situation Habermas describes, like for Rawls, is inconsequential for animals. Non-human interests are mentally unknowable,[287] and generally 'we' cannot 'speak to' or 'for' the interests of nature because nature lacks a formal theory of citizenship.[288] Although we sometimes use stewardship models to represent animal or natural interests, in specific instances these are conflictual between different human lifeworlds of 'folk, agrarian, and industrian'. So, even if we see representation as a common environmental project, ideas will sometimes conflict between 'best' and 'public' interests. Given such plurality, ethical progress might only be made by holding government to account, challenging influential corporations, and transforming traditional laws to deal with the now. So the other parts of procedural ethics are the conditions for community leaders, politicians, and judges to use their legal and political 'Hohfeldian incidents', after Wesley Hohfeld, of *privileges and powers* to make decisions according to, and ultimately shape, *the public interest*. These intractable social conflicts are relatively under-analysed in the one health literature,[289] especially at the level of the theorists' motives to solve public disputes[290] and find the 'common good'.[291] As such, it is not clear how to apply political concepts like 'the public interests' to natural or interspecific interests. Recalling that no framework can absolve any rights, the stage is set, therefore, for an ethical debate about animal rights.

9.5 Rights in Nature

Bernard Williams wrote:

> A central idea in the supposed human prejudice is that there are certain respects in which creatures are treated in one way rather than another simply because they belong to a certain category, the human species. We do not, at this basic initial level, need to know any more about them. Told that there are human beings trapped in a burning building, on the strength of that fact alone we mobilise as many resources as we can to rescue them.[292]

The world is burning.[293] Anthropogenic climate change is devastating human communities *and* environments where animals live. Viruses find these ideal conditions to shatter families and social networks, and meanwhile, an ecological bird flu is ravaging avian populations and will likely spread to ours. Who should be rescued? To be clear, I am not asking whether there are only some humans, or any particular human, who should be saved; remember, one health is not an alternative to public health. The question, therefore, is asked in the abstract.

Perhaps we can start with an idea that individual animals or species are not *necessary* (particularly those that spread disease).[294] If this was the case, then we might simply agree with Williams.

But is that always the case? Firstly, is humanity sustainable without nature? Perhaps we can only imagine nature's end by leaving this world for another planet, but we already know how nature-less places affect us: 'disconnection from nature may have a real and profound impact on our overall well-being'[295] There are the psychological benefits of contact with nature; its absence causes separation anxieties, for example, in Artic bases and space simulation experiments, and cases of 'nature deficit disorder' (which some experienced during the COVID-19 lockdowns). Can we imagine this as a permanent state? Living in cities without access to open and public spaces is systemically unhealthy,[296] which undermines our political and social well-being, too.[297] The reason for saving valuable abstracted natural categories, such as those contained in the UN's Svalbard Global Seed Vault, is that we risk losing vital parts of natural systems, or might use them up, and even miss them when they are gone. But even if we can adapt to potentially calamitous decisions, aren't reincarnated, copied, or surrogate plastic trees and animal animations merely an aesthetic semblance of value? In that future place, there are perhaps fewer opportunities for moral development.[298]

Secondly, underlying this future are the real crimes such as *ecocide* – defined by a biocentric interpretation of widespread damage suffered by entire environments and species.[299] Ironically, the crime is linked to those maximizing their investments to hasten abandonment of a dying world. Even if we get the opportunity to start again in a new place, that opportunity will be for the few, and those survivors are just as likely to take the *ideologies* (the inescapable *noösphere*) into their sovereign biodomes.

And so, to Williams' claim, we can say that if there are *rights in nature*, these cannot be guarded just by assuming *our unique nature*. The non-human dwellers of this planet could have moral considerability, too. And so, consequently, there is, I think, no way yet to tell what one health is: *we do need to know more*.

9.6 Equal Rights, Animal Rights

To answer this one health puzzle, we need to know more about animals. There is recognition of non-human rights in some jurisdictions, but fundamentally, the *idea* of law still divides persons and sorts-of-things:[300] it separates human animals (legal persons) from non-human animals, yet in terms of rights and animal welfare, such a species-restricted definition can be read as 'utilitarianism for animals and Kantianism for humans'.[301] But one health relates to an *anthrozoology* or '*Zoopology*'[302] that plausibly includes exactly the same qualities of humans and non-humans.[303] We need not touch the legal theory that ' . . . so far as the exercise of legal rights is concerned, a person must have a will', but we may reignite the long-standing interest in, 'The Law of modern civilized societies does not recognize animals as the subjects of legal rights. . . . It is quite conceivable, however, that there may have been, or, indeed, may still be, systems of Law in which animals have legal rights, – for instance, cats in ancient Egypt, or white elephants in Siam.'[304]

And so, the only conceivable way to escape bottomless relativity is to address the problematic dichotomies as the 'dialectic structure of reasoning':[305] a method to test bioethical ideas before committing to the real political and social places where choices are made.

As such, we cannot lazily conform to the anthropogenic rights of theme two. So, as Martha Nussbaum argues, we must go further (in animal ethics) using analogical and deductive reasoning thus realizing that Judges must listen to logical argumentation.[306] I agree on the motivation. In Nussbaum's terms, the law is a moral obligation to protect and support the necessary preconditions of *all* life; these conditions are at once specific, transient, and changeable. Nussbaum starts with the human capabilities that we all have, but then she says that animals (could) have many capabilities in common with us. So, although animals cannot 'tell' us their moral interests, we know something fundamental about their rights. From a right *to* place emerges an understanding of the circumstances in which beings can or cannot live, the quality of the climate, opportunities in that place such as land use, and access to fundamental goods such as water and fresh air. She argues that therefore animals – including humans – have *rights to be where they are*.[307] That is also, in principle, sound, insofar as it is a moral, rather than whimsical statement; the latter is indicative of aspirational rendering of international law, but the limits of that belief should be self-evident given the atrocities that awoke human rights in the first place.

But the New York majority's judgement about Happy was not swayed by Nussbaum's *Amicus Brief,* imploring the elephant's transfer from the zoological park to a sanctuary (see Section 8.1).[308] Capabilities do differ between animals (and between individuals of the same species), so we are now talking about the relative ethical weight which leads us onto the tricky ground of 'exotic capabilities'.[309] For the Judges, the unique quality of 'human dignity' sets us apart from nature. So, while Nussbaum rightly says one's changeable nature and place influences one's capabilities, it is a person's *rights* that puts them in 'a place' of absolute security.

If we can reasonably claim there *are moral rights*, then these exist prior to any legal, political, or social recognition.[310] Now, rights presuppose the *principle of equality*: the moral requirement to respect another's intrinsic worth, as ' ... every other being of this kind [has value] and value[s] himself on a footing of equality with them'.[311] Kant is often held to have 'humanized' rights (the *homo phenomenon*), but strictly, rights are held by all rational beings (the *homo noumenon*) or 'beings with wills': 'This holds even if he cannot yet say 'I'; for he still has it in mind. So, any language must think 'I' when it speaks in the first person, even if it has no special word to express it. For this power (the ability to think) is understanding.'[312]

This dialectical approach, based on an internal perspective – here, narrated in summary form,[313] and only meant to provide a scaffold for the third theme of this Element – has an important inference that might prove to be a cornerstone of one health: rights are discovered rather than invented. Unlike the previous two themes, this methodology allows us space to empirically find out if other animals *also* have rights and to do something about it, without relying on certain kinds of socialized perspectives that suggest there is nothing to be discovered. Over the next few pages, this theme will be developed that links a history of rights, the institutions of rights, and the bioethics of rights. If I succeed in my aim, it will be clear that only the latter can provide an anchor for one health practice.

First, then,

'I *know* ... ' (and every rational person *must* know this) ' ... *I have rights*'.[314] Second, 'equality' means that certain resources – generic goods – are indispensable to 'my' well-being, and that are necessary and contextual to other agents. Importantly, this is *not* the subjective claim that we are all born with and have the *same* abilities, *but that we all have objective claims or rights against destitution, poverty, and frustration*. Thus, rights are valid claims to the goods necessary for freedom and well-being: without them, our lives are impoverished by fewer choices and opportunities available; and to make someone worse off in these respects is to treat them without dignity. So, *if* persons are equal in that fashion, then that fulfils the principle of universality: everyone who is a person has rights. And the person 'I am', like all other persons, ' ... ought to do what they logically must accept that they ought to do'.[315]

So, fourthly, in the classical understanding of negative rights – claims to non-interference – *and* socialized positive rights, establish in essence a 'community of rights': an egalitarian place that in and of itself justifies social and welfare opportunities.[316] Finally, I now know, from my conative standpoint, that *no person ought* to live in contexts that, in one health cannon, are called unhealthy environments.

Thus, it behoves us to take seriously the evidence for the rights that another being may have, otherwise we risk excluding them from the community we profess to have self-evident value. For my purpose, it is enough to know that this method is not anthropogenic, as it only depends on the inferences from a first-*person* perspective: if you could ask a chimpanzee (as plausibly a thinking being), they might say, too, that they have no desire to live in squalor. But empirically, it is perhaps enough to observe contexts – based on neurological facts implicit in the dialectical method – to *understand their* plight as a determinant of health.[317]

If (some) animals have rights, then there is a *prima facie* case that the unique contribution of one health ethics is that it is no longer optional to include non-anthropogenic environmental views. In another regard, Roger Brownsword writes: 'We can argue about the details of this context (or commons) but it will include elements pertaining to our wellbeing (clean air and water, food, environmental integrity, and the like) and our freedom (security, an absence of fear and intimidation, and so on).'[318]

I merely add that the commons *is* interspecific. Moreover, in the commons, then, there is an inherent solution to the problems of procedural ethics,[319] because there is a space to ask questions of place and community without risking anyone's rights.[320] Rights already justify procedural ethics (how people *make* laws), on the premise that, even if we cannot possibly hope to agree on substantive issues, we must, morally at least, agree that everyone 'in' has rights.[321] The answers may be evaluatively complex, but need not become circular, because morality, rights, and law have a linear relationship; we can – must – re-evaluate history or change laws, if either do not make sense.[322]

Now, I am going to mention animal rights once more, in respect to the possibility that ' . . . animals have rights, that is, entitlements based on justice to decently flourishing lives'.[323] Our view of rights must ultimately be shaped by awareness of a world that we share with an estimated 8.7 million different species.[324] A tree's biological requirement for rain and ground water is, in many ways, the same as that for a human's basic need for potable water: that connection can also be understood through public bads of pollution or anthropogenic drought. Perhaps nature is also a *universal good* – these goods are similar the 'ecological services' on which all life depends: the land and water are ultimately an ecological determinant of health.[325] Yet such contemplation is obscured in one health cannon and that creates further barriers to realization in enlightened laws and economies.

A tree and a human are not the same morally, although that does not mean that trees have no worth, according to ideas like animism (Latin: *anima* meaning 'breath, spirit, life'), the 'rights of nature', or of 'Mother Nature'. Water is different for aquatic life; here we perceive such extraordinary connection such as that of the blue whale's (*Balaenoptera musculus*) specialist consumption of krill (order *Euphausiacea*), but also the harms that befall this great leviathan as it filters polluted seas and encounters hunters and shipping lanes. There is a stronger case and chance of legal consistency that the blue whale has moral status, which, I think, speaks largely to the progress made in international law.[326] But we also know that much more needs to be done to protect the Cetacea of the seas (as explored in theme two). Their case in international law is not settled. That is because species mean different things: for example, humans, parrots (order *Psittaciformes*), and flying insects, experience spatial freedom, but how each takes up that space affects the other in profoundly different ways due to the properties of hierarchical entities across boundaries, scale, integration, and continuity. These are biological categories, but they are also philosophical relationships – John Locke thought that a talking parrot might be a person;[327] and ethical: birds are threatened by the same flu virus that could wipe out humanity. Over the coming years, we will learn more about the comparative similarities of humans to parrots, gorillas, and blue whales, but this time without invasive dissection. That evidence might inform enlightened policies for insect control and animal vaccination, but that is not all: it will tell us how the bees' intrinsic worth requires protecting them against public bads; and perhaps that worth is more than that of a mosquito. But the point is we have much to learn; and if we rescue nature through reasonable policies, we protect humans, too.

9.7 Reasonable Environmentalism

A connection to nature is often talked about at the fragile frontier of rural communities and traditional knowledge; but it can be found in the environment surrounding everyone and in every community. From the bat-harbouring trees of Méliandou, to the wet markets in Wuhan, the mink farms in Denmark and Spain, and the Bronx Zoo. These connections are the food we eat; the walks we take; in the industries we work for, run or own; and the companions we live with. They are found in sports and services, economies of ecoservices, and a basic living for many people. Everyone is connected to environments in far-off places by trade, work, and tourism.

It is in the universalization of one health that there emerges an argument for *reasonable environmentalism*.[328] Social creatures react to the environment, seek comfortable niches, make changes to places they do not like (or harm us), and create unique cultures and capital to sustain such ways of life in the places that welcome us. There is a distinction with other animals in this regard. As well as the species specific interests, human beings – 'we', 'us' – ideally choose the world that they want to live in; animals will often be stuck where they are. But it is also our imaginations that shape the 'public' environment, the public good and the public interest, on account of such things that 'speak to us'. In our imaginations, the environment can be given *subjective value*, and its various inhabitants different worth depending on their relationship to us, or our knowledge of them; it is such plurality that allows for greater environmental awareness, but also includes fictions that allow some to trample through nature and erode such opportunities.

If we think about fairness in terms of determinants of health, a 'natural' concept of place or space emerges: a place of beings engaged in communication with those willing to listen, and those speaking for those who cannot be heard. Here, then, is where we must also find a *coextensive* place for interspecific justice and for debate.

Reasonableness takes us to the heart of the matter: *ideal* persons (not just legal persons) can agree on empirical facts and interpretations of evidence. They can admit that their knowledge and responses may be fallible (and so that justifies polycentric systems). Yet it is remarkable that contradictions undermine truth and good faith. So, *iff* they are reasonable (that is, can show nonhegemonic philosophic commitments), they must accept the cognitive fact of some form of environmentalism. And, therefore, every reasonable person must care about the life support the planet provides otherwise contradicts that they are affected in any environment.

This sketch is clearly indebted to the giants of rights theory that came before. But even in its rudimentary form, there are two *prudential* arguments for environmentalism: one, that *reasonable* persons should follow a one health approach relative to the benefits and burdens they experience or comprehend (i.e., they are reacting to potential causes of ill health caused by pollution in 'their back yard', even if they cannot empathize with the similar experience of others); and two, even an agnostic would have to concede that connection since they are aware of that 'their' environment is occupied by others who cause pollution or spread a virus.

I do not need to reinvent the wheel in respect to clarifying how these two arguments are moral. Firstly, anyone's actions are universalizable from the prudential point of view, which is to say, their actions cannot be contradictory without suffering some consequential, yet strictly internal 'pain';[329] the egoist is mistaken if they think there is no equality of rights.[330] Yet we know there are certain kinds of anti-environmentalists who, in effect, are making noise that adds up to no argument at all: digging their own graves is a rash if not irrational choice, but it pushes everyone else into conditions of fear, poverty, and adversity. Such actions are antisocial and therefore immoral. And whether they ought to extend concern or help to others in such predicaments is a matter of positive rights, reciprocity, and a duty of rescue (which are another story). But the embarrassment for the antisocial-ist is when their claims do not stack up and are harmfully informed. So, one health should be involved in development of institutions such as courts, fair incentives, and sanctions for 'unreasonableness'. Philosophy can avail us with certain tools in this regard,[331] and the pain of contradiction obviously does not strike terror, so judicial reasons, just as much as fair debate and fact checking, must contribute to forward-looking political movements and reforming governance.

Did one health ethics pass Steven Gould's challenge?

> We are both similar to and different from other animals. In different cultural contexts, emphasis upon one side or the other of this fundamental truth plays a useful social role. In Darwin's day, an assertion of our similarity broke through centuries of harmful superstition. Now we may need to emphasize our difference as flexible animals with a vast range of potential behavior. Our biological nature does not stand in the way of social reform. We are, as Simone de Beauvoir said, 'l'être dont l'être est de n'être pas' – the being whose essence lies in having no essence.[332]

As free thinking, natural beings (is that not our essence?), we ought to attribute freedom and value in the life of others. We do this for countless similar beings by contributing to possible worlds rather than creating inhospitable ones – the one health approach is but one way to do this. But my central claim is that we cannot embark on this journey without first taking the three themes of this Element through a process of reasonableness. Now we know that ethics is not a subterranean theme, but necessary to interpret the historical and legal (and plausibly many other themes); each is part of the process, and together are intellectually compelling reasons to recognize the importance of nature's health, for the simple fact that, for example, we were all exposed to the COVID-19 pandemic, proving that everyone has a direct, transformative connection to nature.

So, finally, I can give one health a definition[a]:

> One health ethics is a theory connecting communities of rights.[b] One health requires that to achieve and maintain social wellbeing, animals[c] will have access to the universal goods of ecosystems, and rights in nature to be free from universal bads.[d]

Notes on this definition:

It is recommended that the reader retrace their steps through this Element to find context for this definition.

a. This definition is justified purely as a normative approach (it is not solely operative). It helps us understand history (see Section 7.), and reasons to redesign institutions (Section 8.); in both respects, one health will be rivalled with principles of public health ethics. The definition is prior to pragmatic solutions for resolving conflicts in the (almost certain) absence of '*common sense*' and that fact, perhaps, suggests why ethics has been peripheral to one health.

b. An ecological or biotic community is a community of rights; a community without or with no nature is a community nowhere (see Section 7.4). An ecological lens distinguishes one health from other anthropocentric health concepts (Section 9.3). Using public health to frame welfare and other opportunities lost to pandemics, often ignores the debate about the rights of non-human animals *also* impacted (Sections 3 and 5). Public health and one health communities can be different; but it is quite reasonable to want to protect one's family – even if they have paws or wings. These animals at least will have interests by virtue of companionship, just as herds have connections to ways of life.[333]

c. A theory of rights does not give *all* animals rights; it is inclusive of human beings (Section 9.7). Strictly, 'humans' or 'animals' have rights as moral agents, which does not mean that other beings have no regard as moral patients.[334] If it is conceivable that (some) animals have rights *of some kind*, then that presupposes one health has a different ethical frame to that of public health. This implies that there will be conflicts as some try to defend absurdities of tradition, the law, etc.

d. The focus of one health ethics is on the *ecological determinants of health* (Section 9.5). These ecological factors are interspecific, so describe the unethical capture of universal goods (Section 9.6). They are part of the web of ethical, legal, social, and political factors that impact on health, but also raise questions of alterity[335] (in respect to making sense of the similar capabilities, responsibilities, needs and circumstances of natural beings, rather than the anthropogenic otherness reflective of public health).

The consequences of environmental neglect are analogous to Gould's *actuality* caused by the threat of nuclear war: we can understand environmental harms as *actual existential* and *non-arbitrary* burdens on communities as meaning the end of society and of nature.[336] So, if this definition is considered a principle (which I hesitate to do, because one must use higher principles to get to this point), then it justifies the importance of animal health for resilient, fair minded communities, situated in places that become less likely to spit out 'nuclear' zoonoses and zooanthroponoses. Reasonable environmentalism, therefore, is coextensive to the goals of a public health theory of healthy populations.

10 Practical One Health

In the final pages of this Element, I will cover some of the implications of *One Health Ethics*, aiming towards what an idea of implementation looks like. I am also aware that time is running out to reach a conclusion. And so, this section will be brief. (In the spirit of a one health, I recognize further interdisciplinary study is needed). What we have found, I think, is that reasonable environmentalism is defensible; but if that explains *one* health, then how can we use it practically and alongside public health? How do we, through our actions and policies, connect *public and interspecific* communities? How do we protect the universal goods of ecosystems, and ensure natural spaces are not subjected to universal bads?

The COVID-19 pandemic showed how every one of us is *in* nature. We are *connected* to and through it: we all caught the virus, including animals, as it circled between the cultural and natural worlds (and, as I have argued, blurred that divide). And we are *of* nature: no one's freedom and well-being were immune to the impacts of the emergent virus (the virus itself, had a 'social life' as it spread from one community to the next). If these impacts are only described as the social determinants of health, then there is a gap in understanding the ecological factors involved.

Now, we can start to explore possibilities for an ethical response to future pandemics by considering the universal goods of ecosystems, the circumstances of environments plagued by poor health, and rescuing environments from public bads. So, how does this change the risks of zoonoses emerging? How do we identify potential pandemic risks? How do we respond to pathogens in our communities? The following are some very broad considerations.

Human rights cannot do all the work for both public health *and* one health. Although we can create a forum to discuss their interests, and that forum must have procedural rules, we must also find a coextensive space for non-human interest. What does public health say about animal rights? Perhaps very little; public health has a specific social, political, and legal outlook that is unconnected to tangible non-human interests.[337]

Keeping all this in mind, one health means that we should look at risk factors *in* human nature *and* subsequently changing frames of international law, subsistence practices, trade and movement, and developing appropriate global surveillance of factors that impact on health and healthy environments. Some of these measures will be controversial, so ethics should be a principal theme: if we adapt 'track and trace' in animal populations then we should be honest about what happens next; culling is rarely justified. If there are ethical alternatives to culling, then we need to change how we think about pandemic preparedness: how do we develop vaccination programmes, or build facilities to quarantine infected animals? Where is the investment to develop treatments (and will) to save animals? Policies should improve animal welfare: if practices are premised on conditions that make animals unhealthy, then ultimately, they risk conditions for diseases to emerge or mutate. We need to build capacity through shared resources such as biobanks, which have conditions of access that allow inter-disciplinary research originating in animal and environmental research questions.[338] But these initiatives should be modelled *for the universal good*, in the same conceptual sense that ethical institutions are resources *for the public good*.[339] That can only be achieved by looking to principles of conservation. We should focus on factors that *cause* pandemics rather than just reacting to public health alerts that come too late: we have a good place to start, by regulating universal bads like pollution and developing adaptations to climate change that consider natural interests. And so, at the highest level, we should look at social capitals that exploit and capture nature:[340] activities that destroy, processes that pollute, policies that displace, and social norms that commodify, are all part of the pandemic story.

The study of reasonable environmentalism throws up these intriguing responses as future directions:

1. Will people follow public health mandates if they *disconnect* them from the nature? During the COVID-19 pandemic, we witnessed the impacts of isolation from the outdoors, and forcing people to pause or sever relationships. Perhaps we saw evidence of a universal shame once we saw it – and a weakening of trust associated with the needless destruction of companion and farm animals.

2. In addition to traditional frames of public engagement, reasonable environmentalists may support public health mandates if there is a rational account of the rights in nature, that is, such that it promotes care of companion animals: these are different cares to those at forefront in public health or economics.

3. Public health seemingly *must* break natural connections (i.e., the epidemiological triad means disrupting at least one causal link between the environment, host, and agent). That singular approach is a result of clinical scope (i.e., to protect in isolation the health of human beings), but becomes illogical if there is a tangible risk/benefit to human populations based on an existential threat to animals.

4. Sharing resources and ideas between public health and conservation and others requires fair consideration of ethical values (which may need changes to law), so that interdisciplinary research leads to mutually beneficial outcomes.
5. Which requires building a catalogue of one health research that defines this *new* ethics, and therefore, tells the story of the opportunities and costs of an ecological approach compared to one based on public health principles.
6. There is scope for approaches that not only integrate complex areas (i.e., genomics), but also change frames of values: for example, Eco(logy) Genomics is a field inspired by the forerunners of the Ethical, Legal, and Social Issues of the Human Genome Project.[341]

Many of these solutions are contentious when looked at from public health; so, let us admit as much when public health, rather than one health, is practised, and tell that alternative story.

And so, I only briefly allude to some of the implications of practising one health ethics.

1. Recognize that some *animals* have rights.
2. In principle, 'one health' communities must challenge the *assumptions* of public health as a unidirectional concept that ignores other forms of well-being (such as the friendship, familial, or spiritual communitarian values that include animals and place).
3. In principle, challenge institutions that disregard (by design) natural risks to the community of rights. Perhaps there are signs of an enlightened environmental policy for them to follow, but the path of an Earth Jurisprudence is not clear.[342] We do not yet know how the international community will respond to the crime of 'ecocide'.

Of course, these few paragraphs barely scratch the surface. But to realize these opportunities, public health must first make space for nature to be part of an evolving community. One health should use that coextensive space to cultivate policies that reflect the idea that we live with, work with, and care for animals.

11 Conclusion

'Questions of the animal origins of human disease lie behind the broadest pattern of human history, and behind some of the most important issues of human health today'.[343] Yet as the COVID-19 pandemic revealed a fragile balance between collectivism and autonomy, individual choice, and social obligation, it also proved there was a brittle ecological relationship between us and nature. And still, there are too few instances of environmentalism to ground evidence-based responses to pandemic preparedness. Nature, after all, is where all future pandemics will start (even if the viral building blocks escape from a lab). Beyond the origin story of COVID-19, the fate of cats, dogs, and mink had little coverage under the din of the vaccine and mask controversies. Even now, the flu pandemic spreading through wild and farmed birds is an ominous reminder that we risk entering again the darkest days of the lockdowns. But when one health appears to call for a new ethics – one that can save wildlife in a way that speaks to our future – it borrows theory to try to square the circle in public health. If public health has never needed a justification more than its purpose of social justice,[344] then why do we need one health? The assumption that I have analysed time and time again, is that public health does all the ethical work for environmentalism. It does not.

The virus was a symptom of the Anthropocene. Despite knowing this, one health has become part of the international response to the climate crisis, yet there seems little impression so far on how it will be a landmark approach. In 1997, Jonathan Mann defined the social determinants of health as the 'societal roots of [public] health problems';[345] under his leadership, ethical responses to AIDS changed policies that for so long had failed to notice the burdens on human rights. Suffice it to say that public health, economics, and law, have not exhausted the opportunities for changing the course of planetary health. They do not have to abandon all their humanism to accept contributions of eco-logical environmentalism, but one health is in theory a view of complex systems of both cultural *and* natural; it is reasonable to suppose, therefore, that one health ethics dissociates argumentation from anti-environmental paradigms, and does not fall into cultural and natural dichotomies, at least, *if we profess to be doing one health.*

One health ethics is not just about rescuing humanity, but about solving the ethical puzzles of a culture disconnecting or leaving behind nature. *One health* is environmentalism: a theory that connects all communities to nature, and a responsibility to recognize and study the connections between the planet's life support system and the environment's cultural value. These are only answerable in a coextensive space for debate. These fora *must* include con-servationists and ecologists as well as others typically left out; there is an obligation to engage with views of a place, built up from years of knowledge and sharing ideas of the land and sea. That is a place connected to all others, just as a pandemic will spread to every corner of the planet. But one health purposes go further: it is a justification for conserving natural places, and it compels us to understand ecological connections in both preservation and restoration of nature. These are ideas we can use to confront the causes of environmental degradation, to make better choices, and ultimately to improve the public's health, too.

Imagining myself looking down upon our colourful rock as it circles the sun, I cannot help but think that there is something that unites *all of us* – it is our rights to enjoy, to wonder at, and wander through nature; and that is where I presume to end this analysis: if we can get the rights, so to speak, right, then one health has an ethical anchor. *One health* is a theory for the betterment of humankind *and* our Earthly companions.[346]

Notes

One Health Environmentalism

1. Crutzen and Stoermer 2000. Unlike previous epochs, the Anthropocene boundary is not evident in the Earth's geology, and is unlikely to be found, yet, so is not formally on the Chronostratigraphic Chart.
2. Wildlife Conservation Society. *One World, One Health: Building Interdisciplinary Bridges to Health in a Globalized World.* The Rockefeller University, New York City, 29th September 2004.
3. Schwabe 1984, 9.
4. Dunlop and Williams 1986, 547, 573, 575.
5. Schwabe 1991.
6. American Veterinary Medical Association 2008, 13.
7. Meadows, et al., 2023.
8. Enserink and Cohen 2009, 1607.
9. Latour 2021a, 2–4.
10. Capps, et al., 2015.
11. Lysaght, et al., 2017.
12. Farmer 2021, xxviii.
13. Steffen, et al., 2007.
14. Blasdell, et al., 2022.
15. *Eco(logical)services* are tangible and intangible benefits that come from ecosystems. These include things that humans need (air, water); services that non-human animals provide, such as pollination; flora that regulates floods and soil erosion; and non-material benefits from nature such as community, recreation, and spirituality. Ecoservices flow back to animal wellbeing.
16. UNEP 2021, 6.
17. Nagle 2009, 78.
18. WHO Director-General's opening remarks at a 'COVID-19' media briefing on 5 May 2023.
19. Ostfeld 2011, 4.
20. Latour 2021b, s26.
21. IPCC 2023, 55.
22. Altizer. et al., 2013.
23. Chan, et al., 2010.
24. Sims, et al., 2003, 832.
25. Montserrat, et al., 2023.
26. O'Neill 2000, 200–202.
27. Capps, et al., 2015, 589.
28. Capps, et al., 2015, 593.
29. Merton 1993, 175–176.
30. Merton 1993, 319.
31. Gould 2002, 1.

32. Gould 2002, 6–7.
33. Sanderson 2002, 162.
34. Latour 2011, 75.
35. Buse, et al., 2019.
36. IPBES 2019, 10, 16.
37. Epstein, et al., 2013.
38. World Bank 2022.
39. Latour 2011, 79–80.
40. de Rosnay 1979, xii.
41. For a review, see Castree 2014.
42. 'The highest form of tradition, by whatever criterion we choose to judge it, is of course human culture. But culture, aside from its involvement with language, which is truly unique, differs from animal tradition only in degree'; Wilson 1975, 168.
43. Descola 2013.
44. Suddendorf 2013.
45. Heath and Rioux 2018.
46. Leopold 1949.
47. Nussbaum 2022; Whitehead and Rendell 2015.
48. Capps 2023.
49. Coggon 2012, 219.
50. O'Neill 1997.
51. Schwabe 1978, 198. Emphasis in original.
52. Allee, et al., 1949.
53. Tansley 1923, 26.
54. Lowe, et al. 2009.
55. Odum 1964.
56. de Rosnay 1979, 223.
57. Coggon 2012, 73.
58. Jennings 2007, 56.
59. Epstein 2004.
60. Faden, et al., 2020.
61. Marí Saéz, et al., 2015. Another story involves an asymptomatic traveller from Sierra Leone, that 'does not negate the possible origins of [Ebola Virus Disease] epidemics in spillover from animal reservoirs, but does demand questioning of the balance between these explanations', Fairhead, et al., 2021, 2.
62. World Health Organization 2014a.
63. Olivero, et al., 2017.
64. Farmer 2021, 453.
65. Farmer 2021, 183, 430.
66. Farmer 2021, xx.
67. Alexander, et al., 2015.
68. Kalema-Zikusoka 2023.
69. For example, the "Realization that veterinary medicine is a human health profession"; Schwabe 1984, 3.

70. Quammen 2012, 116–117.
71. World Health Organization 2014b.
72. Capps and Lederman 2015a.
73. Ryan and Walsh 2011.
74. Leach and Scoones 2013.
75. Morensa, et al., 2020.
76. World Health Organization 2020.
77. World Organisation for Animal Health 2022.
78. Lederman, et al., 2021.
79. Zinsstag, et al., 2023.
80. Capps, et al., 2015.
81. Langton, et al., 2022.
82. Searle and Turnbull 2020, 294.
83. Rutz, et al., 2020.
84. Latour 2021b, s26.
85. Häsler, et al., 2014.
86. E.g., Friese and Nuyts 2017, 304.
87. In comparison, Paul Farmer's (1959–2022) *Fevers, Feuds, and Diamonds* needs 653 pages to tell the story of Ebola in Africa; Farmer 2021, 430. Calvin Schwabe similarly relates colonialism to the development of veterinary public health; Schwabe 1998.
88. Gudynas 2011.
89. Majok and Schwabe 1996, 15.
90. Unknown Author 1814, 58.
91. Rush 1811, 297.
92. Rush 1811, 296.
93. Rush 1811, 313.
94. Rush 1811, 302.
95. Virchow is 'frequently quoted, in the absence of any identifiable [or primary] source material' as the originator of One Medicine; Woods, et al., 2018, 15.
96. Saunders 2000, 203. The quote is apparently taken from (I have not attempted to re-translate): Bollinger, O. Über die Bedeutung der Thiermedicin und der Vergleichenden Pathologie. *Deutsche Zeitschrift für Thiermedicin und Vergleichende Pathologie* 1 (1875): 7–23.
97. No author 1876, 465–466.
98. Unknown Author 1814, 167. Also see, Rush 1809.
99. Fairbanks 2020.
100. No author 1882.
101. Osler 1904.
102. Virchow 1881, 203.
103. Paget 1902, 117. Osler died of 'Spanish flu' in 1919; he was one of 50 million deaths from the pandemic that was probably avian in origin – an ironic coda in that part of the story of one health.
104. Moore 1923, 293.
105. Klauder 1958, 170.

106. Klauder 1958, 171.
107. Quoted in, Beerman 1968. From an original concept by, Mueller, H. Veterinary Medicine at Crossroads. *Der Praktische Tierarzt* (1954) 4: 53–55. I was not able to access this article.
108. Perry and Perry 1914, vii.
109. Perry and Perry 1914, 55.
110. Schmidt 1962, 903–904.
111. Editorial 1975, 535.
112. Cassidy 2017, 204.
113. Schwabe 1978, 171.
114. Schwabe 1984.
115. Schwabe 1984, 3.
116. Schwabe 1984, 3.
117. Schwabe 1984, 2.
118. Schwabe 1984, 2.
119. Association of Teachers of Veterinary Public Health and Preventive Medicine Newsletter, Spring /Summer, 2002, 3.
120. Schwabe 1993, 5.
121. Schwabe 1991.
122. Rodriguez 2012, vii.
123. Kock 1996.
124. Horton and Lo 2015.
125. Whitmee, et al., 2015.
126. Smith, et al., 2018, 634.
127. Brandi 2015.
128. Kock 2003, 11.
129. Karesh 1999, 10.
130. Weiss, 2003.
131. Osofsky, et al., 2003, 2.
132. Karesh, et al., 2002.
133. Goodall 1983.
134. Wolfe, et al. 1998, 155.
135. See *supra* note 2.
136. Osofsky, et al., 2005, 68.
137. Zinsstag, et al., 2005.
138. Bresalier, et al., 2020, 8.
139. FAO, et al., 2008, 5.
140. FAO, et al., 2010.
141. American Veterinary Medical Association 2008.
142. Gruetzmacher, et al., 2021.
143. Based on a study by, Lysaght, et al., 2017.
144. OHHLEP 2022, 11.
145. Schwabe 1998, 121.
146. Mwatondo, et al., 2023.
147. Porter 2000, 3.
148. Latour 2011, 77.

149. Harrison 1992, 227.
150. Hobbes 2005, 111.
151. Beyleveld and Brownsword 2007, 328.
152. Locke 1975, 517.
153. Hume 1962, 227.
154. Kant 1974, 3.
155. O'Neill 1998.
156. 'It could well be that some other planet is inhabited by rational beings who have to think aloud – who, whether awake or dreaming, in company with others or alone, can have no thoughts they do not utter. How would their behavior toward one another then differ from that of the human race?'; Kant 1974, 192.
157. Bentham 1823, 310–311.
158. Mill 1957, 10.
159. Desmond and Moore 2009, 243–244.
160. Desmond and Moore 2009, 252.
161. Desmond and Moore 2009, 260.
162. Medvedyuk, et al., 2021.
163. Rome 2003, 526.
164. Crutzen 2002.
165. Teilhard de Chardin 1966, 80.
166. Vernadsky 1998.
167. Porter 2003, xvi.
168. Latour 2011, 73.
169. UN 2021.
170. Lenton and Latour 2018, 1067.
171. See, Capps 2009.
172. Kirby 2010.
173. UN 2021.
174. Jennings 2007, 31. There is a body of work that suggests relative cultural-based approaches may not be ethical, let alone successfully universalised; Kerby 2010.
175. Human biology is not what grounds the relationship between rights and dignity, which, as we shall see, needs reconsideration in the law of animals; Beyleveld and Brownsword 2001, 210.
176. Barugahare 2018, 4.
177. Gudynas 2011, 441.
178. Gudynas 2018.
179. Sen 1997.
180. Nusbaum 2022.
181. Waldron 2009, 22.
182. Beyleveld and Brownsword 1986.
183. Annas 1998, 1780.
184. Garcia and Gostin 2012.
185. Beitz 2011.
186. CBD/COP/15/L.25; 18 December 2022.

187. Nusbaum 2022, 301.

188. Wolfrum and Matz, 2000.

189. Animals are protected under different standards of animal welfare, but that is a jurisdictional matter as well as theoretical task beyond this Element; see, Garner 2013.

190. A/CONF.232/2023/4, 19–20 June, 2023.

191. UN 2000.

192. No Author 2001.

193. Macpherson 2007, 588.

194. Nonhuman Rights Project 2022, 2.

195. Nonhuman Rights Project 2022, 15. Dichotomous reasoning also means that some 'human beings' are excluded from the scope of international law; a conflation that was not noticed at the time since abstraction was made from (possibly) different first principles. That is, it does not preclude pregnancy termination (i.e., because of when life starts, see: Vo v. France (Application no 53924/00) (2024), or human embryo research (e.g., the European Convention on Human Rights and Biomedicine creates a specific problem of how to read 'everyone' and 'human being'; they cannot be the same; Capps 2003, 158–162). Arguments about life and potential life remain controversial, with more recent reproductive cases being circumspect about human rights being factually held by *all* human life; See M.L. v. Poland (Application no. 40119/21) (2023); and Parrillo v. Italy (Application no. 46470/11) (2015). All cases are from the European Court of Human Rights.

196. OHHLEP 2022, 12.

197. UN 2015.

198. Pinter, et al., 2015, v., 38.

199. Pinter, et al., 2015, 1.

200. Sachs, et al., 2021.

201. ICS/ISSC 2015, 9.

202. Spaiser, et al., 2017, 468.

203. Lenton and Latour 2018, 1067.

204. FAO, et al., 2022, 49.

205. FAO, et al., 2022, 49.

206. For example, on economic language as the dominant language in social science discourse, see, Lowi 1992.

207. United Nations' High-Level Expert Group on the Net Zero Emissions Commitments of Non-State Entities 2022.

208. McGraw 2013; UN 2010.

209. Compare, Lutz 1999, 258–259.

210. Gallo-Cajiao, et al., 2023, e337.

211. McCloskey 1989, 226.

212. Heath 2022, 2.

213. Bali, et al., 2022, 7.

214. *Social capital* is defined by its production of ethical activities; a society's interests – through mutual acquaintance or recognition – creates resources

that can be used for defined obligations/desired outcomes; see Capps 2017.

215. 'This [one health] Operational Framework presents a multi-sectoral approach to reconcile, connect, and develop synergies and efficiencies, strengthen human and animal public health systems, and ultimately protect global public goods, while preserving ecosystems and ensuring a more equitable distribution of health gains' (World Bank 2022, 2).
216. Johnson, et al., 2016.
217. Lutz 1999.
218. Stone 1972, 498.
219. Navarro 2004, 673.
220. Wallace, et al., 2015.
221. Kruse 2019.
222. Rawls 1971, 3.
223. Latour 2004a, 462.
224. Latour 2004b, 226. Italics in original.
225. Latour 1991, 142.
226. Latour 2011, 73. Italics in original.
227. Fang 2010.
228. Carson 1962.
229. Janousek, et al., 2023.
230. Goulson 2021.
231. Warner 2018.
232. Capps 2019.
233. MacGregor and Waldman 2017, 3.
234. Hollis and Nell 1975, 264.
235. Gould 1984.
236. FAO, et al., 2022, xi.
237. Brabazon 2000.
238. Leopold 1949, 211, 224–225.
239. Næss 1989.
240. Warren 1983, 130–131.
241. Taylor 1986.
242. Regan 1983.
243. Midgley 1978, xiii
244. Rolston 1975, 105.
245. *credible.
246. Smil 2002, 265.
247. Heath 2022.
248. Sanderson 2002, 163.
249. Chien 2013, 215.
250. Spencer, et al., 2019, 2.
251. Mwatondo, et al., 2023, 611
252. Coggon 2012, 215.
253. 'OneHealth may offer an inspiring and fruitful perspective, but as a concept it is inevitably all encompassing and broad, and therefore

risks having relatively little meaningful or distinctive content'; Verweij and Bovenkerk 2016, 2.

254. 'After all, practitioners rather than philosophers may be better placed to understand the political and strategic climate in which public health decision making operates'; Johnson and Degeling 2019, 142.

255. Chien 2013, 220.

256. Chien 2013, 219.

257. Degeling, et al., 2019, 68. Citations omitted.

258. Sass 2007.

259. Steger 2015, 216.

260. Potter 1988, 74.

261. See, Thomas Taylor's response to Mary Wollstonecraft's (1759–1797) *Vindication of the Rights of Women* (1792). In his *A Vindication of the Rights of Brutes* he mocked the absurd consequences of giving animals rights; Taylor 1966.

262. We cannot live by the laws of nature like 'bees or ants'! Hobbes 2005, 135.

263. Donagan 1977, 171.

264. Krieger 1973, 453.

265. Black, et al. 1982.

266. Schwabe 1984, 2.

267. Morton 2007, 9.

268. Tarlock 2004.

269. Coggon 2012, 207. Italics in original.

270. Callicott 2013, 54.

271. Coggon 2012, 247.

272. Coggon 2012, 253.

273. Brookes, et al., 2010.

274. Ostrom 2010.

275. Dietz, et al., 2002.

276. Ostrom 2007. Norms are developed by publics (where sociality, economies, and laws merge with one another), studied by academics, used by politicians, and applied by judges; they tell us about who participates, what topics are on the table, and the available solutions.

277. McCarthy 1973.

278. Capps 2008.

279. Richard Sylvan (Routley) advocated for *biospherical egalitarianism* – 'the equal value of all life'; Routley 1973, 210.

280. Latour 2011, 79.

281. Lynas, et al., 2021.

282. Capps 2019.

283. Degeling, et al., 2019, 74.

284. Cohen 1986, 868.

285. Schwabe 1991, 942.

286. Szasz 1969, 242.

287. Nagel 1974.

288. Donaldson and Kymlicka 2011.

289. Capps 2019.
290. Durrant 2011.
291. Hollis 1996, 168.
292. Williams 2006, 142.
293. Lohman, et al., 2007.
294. See the example in Law 2008.
295. Neilson, et al., 2021, 2.
296. Bratman, et al., 2019.
297. Capps 2013a.
298. Zwarthoed 2016.
299. Stop Ecocide Foundation 2021, 2.a.ii.
300. Wise 2000.
301. Garner 2013.
302. Esbjörn-Hargens and Zimmerman 2009, 562.
303. Sanders and Arluke 1993.
304. Grey 1909, 42.
305. Selter and Salloch 2023, 8.
306. Nussbaum 2022.
307. Nussbaum 2022, 114.
308. Nussbaum 2020.
309. Claassen and Düwell 2013, 506.
310. Capps and Pattinson 2017.
311. Kant 1974, 9.
312. Kant 1996, 186.
313. Gewirth 1978.
314. This is said prior to anyone taking or violating my rights, and in the sense that am I not going to say the opposite in such circumstances (and neither can they) – "I have no rights!".
315. This argument paraphrases Alan Gewirth's *Reason and Morality*. Gewirth 1978, 153.
316. Gewirth 1996, 31–32.
317. Capps 2023.
318. Brownsword 2009, 225.
319. Capps 2019.
320. Capps 2021.
321. Capps 2008.
322. Gewirth 1973.
323. Nussbaum 2022, xxv.
324. Mora, et al., 2011.
325. Capps and Lederman 2015b.
326. Nussbaum and Nussbaum 2016.
327. Locke 1975, 2.27.8.
328. Capps 2022a. The following paragraph is a summary.
329. Gewirth 1978, 135.
330. O'Neill 1997.
331. Capps 2022b.

332. Gould 1978, 350–351.
333. Majok and Schwabe 1996.
334. Pluhar 1988.
335. Toddington 2013.
336. Gewirth 1986.
337. Coggon 2012.
338. Capps and Lederman 2015b.
339. Capps 2013b.
340. Capps 2017.
341. Capps, et al., 2023.
342. UN 2019.
343. Diamond 1997, 197.
344. Lee 2017.
345. Mann 1997.
346. Capps 2021, 348.

References

Alexander, Kathleen, Sanderson, Claire, Marathe, Madav, et al. What Factors Might Have Led to the Emergence of Ebola in West Africa? *PLoS Neglected Tropical Diseases* 9(6) (2015): e0003652.

Allee, Warder, Emerson, Alfred, Park, Thomas, Park, Orlando, Schmidt, Karl. *Principles of Animal Ecology*. Philadelphia: B. Saunders, 1949.

Altizer, Sonia, Ostfeld, Richard, Johnson, Pieter, Kutz, Susan, Harvell, Drew. Climate Change and Infectious Diseases: From Evidence to a Predictive Framework. *Science* 341 (2013): 514–19.

American Veterinary Medical Association. *One Health: A New Professional Imperative*. One Health Initiative Task Force: Final Report. July 15. Schaumburg: American Veterinary Medical Association, 2008.

Annas, George. Human Rights and Health – The Universal Declaration of Rights at 50. *New England Journal of Medicine* 339 (1998): 1778–81.

Bali, Sulzhan, Batmanian, Garo, Berthe, Franck. *Putting Pandemics Behind Us: Investing in One Health to Reduce Risks of Emerging Infectious Diseases*. Washington, DC: International Bank for Reconstruction and Development/ The World Bank, 2022.

Barugahare, John. African Bioethics: Methodological Doubts and Insights. *BMC Medical Ethics* 19 (2018): 98.

Beerman, Herman. Perspectives in Comparative Dermatology: William Allen Pusey Memorial Address. *Archives of Dermatology* 98 (1968): 400–5.

Beitz, Charles. *The Idea of Human Rights*. New York: Oxford University Press, 2011.

Bentham, Jeremy. *An Introduction to the Principles of Morals and Legislation*. Oxford: Clarendon Press, 1823.

Beyleveld, Deryck, Brownsword, Roger. *Law as a Moral Judgment*. Sheffield: Sheffield Academic, 1986.

Beyleveld, Deryck, Brownsword, Roger. *Human Dignity in Bioethics and Biolaw*. Oxford: Oxford University Press, 2001.

Beyleveld, Deryck, Brownsword, Roger. *Consent in the Law*. Oxford: Hart, 2007.

Black, Douglas, Smith, Cyril, Townsend, Peter. *Inequalities in Health: The Black Report*. New York: Penguin Books, 1982.

Blasdell, Kim, Morand, Serge, Laurance, Susan, Firth, Cadhla. Rats and the City: Implications of Urbanization on Zoonotic Disease Risk in Southeast

Asia. *Proceedings of the National Academies of Science* 119 (2022): e2112341119.

Brabazon, James. *Albert Schweitzer: A Biography.* Syracuse: Syracuse University Press, 2000.

Brandi, Clara. Safeguarding the Earth System as a Priority for Sustainable Development and Global Ethics: The Need for an Earth System SDG. *Journal of Global Ethics* 11 (2015): 32–36.

Bratman, Gregory, Anderson, Christopher, Berman, Marc, et al. Nature and Mental Health: An Ecosystem Service Perspective. *Science Advances* 5 (2019). https://doi.org/10.1126/sciadv.aax0903.

Bresalier, Michael, Cassidy, Angela, Woods, Abigail. One Health in History. In Zinsstag, Jakob, Schelling, Esther, Crump, Lisa, et al. *One Health: The Theory and Practice of Integrated Health Approaches.* 2nd ed. Wallingford: CAB International, 2020: 1–14.

Brookes, Victoria, Ward, Michael, Rock, Melanie, Degeling, Chris. One Health Promotion and the Politics of Dog Management in Remote, Northern Australian Communities. *Scientific Reports* 10 (2010): 12451.

Brownsword, Roger. Friends, Romans, and Countrymen: Is There a Universal Right to Identity? *Law, Innovation and Technology* 1 (2009): 223–49.

Buse, Chris, Smith, Maxwell, Silva, Diego. Attending to Scalar Ethical Issues in Emerging Approaches to Environmental Health Research and Practice. *Monash Bioethics Review* 37 (2019): 4–21.

Callicott, Bard. *Thinking Like a Planet: The Land Ethic and the Earth Ethic.* Oxford: Oxford University Press, 2013.

Capps, Benjamin. Authoritative Regulation and the Stem Cell Debate. *Bioethics* 22 (2008): 43–55.

Capps, Benjamin. Defining Variables of Access to UK Biobank: The Public Interest and the Public Good. *Law, Innovation and Technology* 5 (2013b): 113–39.

Capps, Benjamin. Gene Drive Gone Wild: Exploring Deliberative Possibilities by Developing One Health Ethics. *Law, Innovation and Technology* 11 (2019): 231–56.

Capps, Benjamin. One Health Ethics. *Bioethics* 36 (2022a): 348–55.

Capps, Benjamin. One Health Requires a Theory of Agency. *Cambridge Quarterly of Healthcare Ethics* 31 (2022b): 518–29.

Capps, Benjamin. Privacy, Rights and Biomedical Data Collections. In Kaan, Terry, and Ho, Calvin, eds. *Genetic Privacy in Singapore: Science, Ethics and Law.* Singapore: World Scientific, 2013a: 69–202.

Capps, Benjamin. *UK and European Policy in Stem Cell Research: Proposals for the Ethical Grounding of Future Regulation.* Bristol: University of Bristol, 2003.

Capps, Benjamin. Authoritative Regulation and the Stem Cell Debate. *Bioethics.* 22 (2008): 43–55.

Capps, Benjamin. Privacy, Rights and Biomedical Data Collections. In Kaan, Terry, and Ho, Calvin, eds. *Genetic Privacy in Singapore: Science, Ethics and Law.* Singapore: World Scientific, 2013a: 69–202.

Capps, Benjamin. Defining Variables of Access to UK Biobank: The Public Interest and the Public Good. *Law, Innovation and Technology,* 5 (2013b): 113–39.

Capps, Benjamin. Public Goods in the Ethical Reconsideration of Research Innovation. In Capps, Patrick, and Patterson, Shaun, eds. *Ethical Rationalism and the Law.* Oxford: Hart, 2017: 149–69.

Capps, Benjamin. Gene Drive Gone Wild: Exploring Deliberative Possibilities by Developing One Health Ethics. *Law, Innovation and Technology,* 11 (2019): 231–56.

Capps, Benjamin. Where Does Open Science Lead Us During a Pandemic? A Public Good Argument to Prioritise Rights in the Open Commons. *Cambridge Quarterly of Healthcare Ethics* 30 (2021): 1–14.

Capps, Benjamin. One Health Ethics. *Bioethics* 36 (2022a): 348–55.

Capps, Benjamin. One Health Requires a Theory of Agency. *Cambridge Quarterly of Healthcare Ethics* 31 (2022b): 518–29.

Capps, Benjamin. What Do Chimeras Think about? *Cambridge Quarterly of Healthcare Ethics* 32 (2023): 496–514.

Capps, Benjamin, Bailey, Michele, Bickford, David. et al. Introducing One Health to the Ethical Debate about Zoonotic Diseases in South East Asia. *Bioethics* 29 (2015): 588–96.

Capps, Benjamin, Lederman, Zohar. One Health, Vaccines and Ebola: The Opportunities for Shared Benefits. *Journal of Agriculture and Environmental Ethics* 28 (2015a): 1011–32.

Capps, Benjamin, Lederman, Zohar. One Health and Paradigms of Public Biobanking. *Journal of Medical Ethics* 41 (2015b): 258–62.

Capps, Benjamin, Chadwick, Ruth, Lederman, Zohar, et al. The Human Genome Organisation (HUGO) and a Vision for Ecogenomics: The Ecological Genome Project. *Human Genomics* 17 (2023).

Capps, Patrick. *Human Dignity and the Foundations of International Law.* Oxford: Hart, 2009.

Capps, Patrick, Pattinson, Shaun. The Past, Present and Future of Ethical Rationalism. In Capps, Patrick, and Patterson, Shaun, eds. *Ethical Rationalism and the Law*. Oxford: Hart, 2017: 1–16.

Carson, Rachel. *Silent Spring*. Boston: Houghton Mifflin, 1962.

Cassidy, Angela. Humans, Other Animals and 'One Health' in the Early Twenty-First Century. In Woods, Abigail, Bresalier, Michael, Cassidy, Angela, and Dentinger, Rachel, eds. *Animals and the Shaping of Modern Medicine*. London: Palgrave Macmillan, 2017: 193–245.

Castree, Noel. *Making Sense of Nature*. New York: Routledge, 2014.

Chan, Emily, Brewer, Timothy, Madoff, Lawrence, et al. Global Capacity for Emerging Infectious Disease Detection. *Proceedings of the National Academy of Sciences* 107 (2010): 21701–6.

Chien, Yu-Ju. How Did International Agencies Perceive the Avian Influenza Problem? The Adoption and Manufacture of the 'One World, One Health' Framework. *Sociology of Health & Illness* 35 (2013): 213–26.

Claassen, Rutger, Düwell, Marcus. The Foundations of Capability Theory: Comparing Nussbaum and Gewirth. *Ethical Theory and Moral Practice* 16 (2013): 493–510.

Coggon, John. *What Makes Health Public?* Cambridge: Cambridge University Press, 2012.

Cohen, Carl. The Case for Biomedical Experimentation. *New England Journal of Medicine* 315 (1986): 865–70.

Crutzen, Paul, Stoermer, Eugene. The 'Anthropocene'. *IGBP Newsletter* 41 (2000): 17–18.

Crutzen, Paul. Geology of Mankind. *Nature* 415 (2002): 23.

Degeling, Chris, Dawson, Angus, Gilbert, Gwendolyn. The Ethics of One Health. In Walton, Merrilyn, ed. *One Planet, One Health*. Sydney: Sydney University Press, 2019: 65–84.

de Rosnay, Joël. *The Macroscope: A New World Scientific System*. New York: Harper & Row, 1979.

Descola, Philippe. *Beyond Nature and Culture*. Translated by Janet Lloyd. Chicago: Chicago University Press, 2013.

Desmond, Adrian, Moore, James. *Darwin*. London: Penguin Books, 2009.

Diamond, Jared. *Guns, Germs and Steel*. New York: W.W. Norton, 1997.

Dietz, Thomas, Dolšak, Nives, Ostrom, Elinor, Stern, Paul. The Drama of the Commons. In Ostrom, Elinor, Dietz, Thomas, Dolšak, Nives, et al., eds. *The Drama of the Commons*. Washington, DC: The National Academies Press, 2002: 3–35.

Donagan, Alan. *The Theory of Morality*. Chicago: University of Chicago Press, 1977.

Donaldson, Sue, Kymlicka, Will. *Zoopolis: A Political Theory of Animal Rights*. Oxford: Oxford University Press, 2011.

Dunlop, Robert, Williams, David. *Veterinary Medicine: An Illustrated History*. St. Louis: Mosby-Year Book, 1986.

Durant, Darrin. Models of Democracy in Social Studies of Science. *Social Studies of Science* 41 (2011): 691–714.

Editorial. Two Disciplines, One Medicine. *Veterinary Record* 96 (1975): 535.

Enserink, Martin, Cohen, Jon. The Novel H1N1 Influenza. *Science* 326 (2009): 1607.

Epstein, Graham, Vogt, Jessica, Mincey, Sarah, Cox, Michael, Fischer, Burney. Missing Ecology: Integrating Ecological Perspectives with the Social-Ecological System Framework. *International Journal of the Commons* 7 (2013): 432–53.

Epstein, Richard. In Defense of the 'Old' Public Health. *Brooklyn Law Review* 69 (2004): 1421–70.

Esbjörn-Hargens, Sean, Zimmerman, Michael. *Integral Ecology: Uniting Multiple Perspectives on the Natural World*. Boston: Integral Books, 2009.

Faden, Ruth, Bernstein, Justine, Shebaya, Sirine. Public Health Ethics. In Zalta, Edward, ed. *The Stanford Encyclopedia of Philosophy* (Fall ed.) (2020). https://plato.stanford.edu/archives/fall2020/entries/publichealth-ethics/

Fairbanks, Daniel. Mendel and Darwin: Untangling a Persistent Enigma. *Heredity* 124 (2020): 263–73.

Fairhead, James, Leach, Melissa, Millimouno, Dominique. Spillover or Endemic? Reconsidering the Origins of Ebola Virus Disease Outbreaks by Revisiting Local Accounts in Light of New Evidence from Guinea. *BMJ Global Health* 6 (2021): e005783.

Fang, Janet. Ecology: A World Without Mosquitoes. *Nature* 466 (2010): 432–34.

Farmer, Paul. *Fevers, Feuds, and Diamonds: Ebola and the Ravages of History*. New York: Picador, 2021.

Food and Agriculture Organization (FAO), the United Nations Environment Programme (UNEP), the World Organisation for Animal Health (WOAH), and the World Health Organization (WHO). *One Health Joint Plan of Action (2022–2026): Working together for the Health of Humans, Animals, Plants and the Environment*. Rome: FAO, UNEP, WHO & WOAH, 2022.

Food and Agriculture Organization (FAO), World Organization for Animal Health (OIE), World Health Organization (WHO). The FAO-OIE-WHO Collaboration: *Sharing Responsibilities and Coordinating Global Activities to Address Health Risks at the Animal-Human-Ecosystems Interfaces: A Tripartite Concept Note*. April, 2010.

Food and Agriculture Organization (FAO), World Organization for Animal Health (OIE), World Health Organization (WHO), United Nations Children's Fund (UNICEF), the World Bank, and UN System Influenza Coordinator (UNSIC). *Contributing to One World, One Health: A Strategic Framework for Reducing Risks of Infectious Diseases at the Animal–Human–Ecosystems Interface.* October, 2008.

Friese, Carrie, Nuyts, Nathalie. Posthumanist Critique and Human Health: How Nonhumans (Could) Figure in Public Health Research. *Critical Public Health* 27 (2017): 303–13.

Gallo-Cajiao, Eduardo, Lieberman, Susan, Dolšak, Nives, et al. Global Governance for Pandemic Prevention and the Wildlife Trade. *Lancet Planetary Health* 7 (2023): e336–e345.

Garcia, Kelli, Gostin, Lawrence. One Health, One World – The Intersecting Legal Regimes of Trade, Climate Change, Food Security, Humanitarian Crises, and Migration. *Laws* 1 (2012): 4–38.

Garner, Robert. *A Theory of Justice for Animals.* Oxford: Oxford University Press, 2013.

Gewirth, Alan. The 'Is-Ought' Problem Resolved. *Proceedings and Addresses of the American Philosophical Association* 47 (1973): 34–61.

Gewirth, Alan. *Reason and Morality.* Chicago: Chicago University Press, 1978.

Gewirth, Alan. Reason and Nuclear Deterrence. *Canadian Journal of Philosophy* 16 (1986): 129–59.

Gewirth, Alan. *The Community of Rights.* Chicago: Chicago University Press, 1996.

Goodall, Jane. Population Dynamics During a 15 Year Period in one Community of Free-Living Chimpanzees in the Gombe National Park, Tanzania. *Zeitschrift für Tierpsychologie* 61 (1983): 1–60.

Gould, Stephen. Sex, Drugs, Disasters, and the Extinction of Dinosaurs. *Discover* March (1984): 67–72.

Gould, Stephen. *The Structure of Evolutionary Theory.* Cambridge Harvard University Press, 2002.

Gould, Stephen. Biological Potential vs. Biological Determinism. In Caplan, Arthur, ed., *The Sociobiology Debate.* New York: Harper & Row, 1978: 343–51.

Goulson, Dave. *Silent Earth: Averting the Insect Apocalypse.* London: Jonathan Cape, 2021.

Gray, John. *The Nature and Sources of the Law.* New York: Columbia University Press, 1909.

Gruetzmacher, Kim, Karesh, William, Amuasi, John, et al. The Berlin Principles on One Health – Bridging Global Health and Conservation. *Science of the Total Environment* 764 (2021): 142919.

Gudynas, Eduardo. Buen Vivir: Today's Tomorrow. *Development* 54 (2011): 441–47.

Gudynas, Eduardo. Contribution to GTI Roundtable Vivir Bien: An Exchange on the Essay Vivir Bien: Old Cosmovisions and New Paradigms. *Great Transition Initiative* February (2018): www.greattransition.org/roundtable/vivir-bien-eduardo-gudynas.

Harrison, Peter. Descartes on Animals. *The Philosophical Quarterly* 42 (1992): 219–27.

Häsler, Barbara, Hiby, Elly, Gilbert, Will, et al. A One Health Framework for the Evaluation of Rabies Control Programmes: A Case Study from Colombo City, Sri Lanka. *PLoS Neglected Tropical Diseases* 8 (2014): e3270.

Heath, Joseph. The Failure of Traditional Environmental Philosophy. *Res Publica* 28 (2022): 1–16.

Heath, Joseph, Rioux, Catherine. Recent Trends in Evolutionary Ethics: Greenbeards! *Biology & Philosophy* 33 (2018): 16.

Hobbes, Thomas. *Leviathan*. A critical edition by Rogers, G. and Schuhmann, Karl. Volume Two. London: Continuum International Publishing Group, 2005 (original 1651).

Hollis, Martin. *Reason in Action*. Cambridge: Cambridge University Press, 1996.

Hollis, Martin, Nell, Edward. *Rational Economic Man: A Philosophical Critique of Neo-Classical Economics*. Cambridge: Cambridge University Press, 1975.

Horton, Richard, Lo, Selina. Planetary Health: A New Science for Exceptional Action. *Lancet* 386 (2015): 1921–22.

Hume, David. *A Treatise of Human Nature: Book 1*. Macnabb, D. ed. London: Fontana Library, 1962 (original 1739).

Intergovernmental Panel on Climate Change (IPCC). *Climate Change 2023: Synthesis Report*. Geneva: IPCC, 2023.

Intergovernmental Science-Policy Platform on Biodiversity and Ecosystem Services (IPBES). *The Global Assessment Report on Biodiversity and Ecosystem Services*. Bonn: IPBES Secretariat, 2019.

International Council for Science (ICS) and International Social Science Council (ISSC). *Report: Review of Targets for the Sustainable Development Goals: The Science Perspective*. Paris: International Council for Science, 2015.

Janousek, William, Douglas, Margaret, Cannings, Syd, et al. Recent and Future Declines of a Historically Widespread Pollinator Linked to Climate, Land Cover, and Pesticides. *Proceedings of the National Academy of Sciences* 120 (2023): e2211223120.

Jennings, Bruce. Public Health and Civic Republicanism. In Dawson, Angus, and Verweij, Marcel, eds. *Ethics, Prevention, and Public Health*. Oxford: Oxford University Press, 2007: 30–58.

Johnson, Hope, South, Nigel, Walters, Reece. Eco-Crime and Fresh Water. In Hall, Matthew, Maher, Jennifer, Nurse, Angus, et al., eds. *Greening Criminology in the 21st Century Edition*. London: Routledge, 2016: 133–46.

Johnson, Jane, Degeling, Chris. Does One Health Require a Novel Ethical Framework? *Journal of Medical Ethics* 45 (2019): 239–43.

Kalema-Zikusoka, Gladys. *Walking with Gorillas: The Journey of an African Wildlife Vet*. New York: Arcade, 2023.

Kant, Immanuel. *Anthropology from a Pragmatic Point of View*. Translated, with an Introduction by Gregor, Mary. The Hague: Martinus Nijhoff, 1974 (original 1798).

Kant, Immanuel. *The Metaphysics of Morals*. Gregor, Mary, ed. Cambridge: Cambridge University Press, 1996 (original 1797).

Karesh, William. *Appointment at the Ends of the World: Memoirs of a Wildlife Veterinarian*. New York: Warner Books, 1999.

Karesh, William, Osofsky, Steven, Rocke, Tonie, Barrows, Paul. Joining Forces to Improve Our World. *Conservation Biology* 16 (2002): 1432–34.

Kirby, Michael. Health Care and Global Justice. *Singapore Academy of Law Journal* 22 (2010): 785–800.

Klauder, Joseph. Interrelations of Human and Veterinary Medicine: Discussion on Some Aspects of Comparative Dermatology. *New England Journal of Medicine* 258 (1958) 170–77.

Kock, Micheal. The Health Paradigm and Disease Control: Consideration of the Health of Ecosystems and Impacts on Human Health and Rural Livelihoods [Abstract]. *AHEAD Invitees' Briefing Packet. Southern and East African Experts Panel on Designing Successful Conservation and Development Interventions at the Wildlife/Livestock Interface: Implications for Wildlife, Livestock, and Human Health. Animal Health for the Environment and Development.* IUCN Vth World Parks Congress 14–15 September, Durban, 2003.

Kock, M. D. Wildlife, People and Development: Veterinary Contributions to Wildlife Health and Resource Management in Africa. *Tropical Animal Health and Production* 28 (1996): 68–80.

Krieger, Martin. What's Wrong with Plastic Trees? *Science* 179 (1973): 446–55.

Kruse, Marion. Ecosystem Health Indicators. *Encyclopedia of Ecology (2nd ed.)* 1 (2019): 407–14.

Latour, Bruno. *We Have Never Been Modern*. Cambridge: Harvard University Press, 1991.

Latour, Bruno. Whose Cosmos, Which Cosmopolitics? Symposium: Talking Peace with Gods, Part 1. *Common Knowledge* 10 (2004a): 450–62.

Latour, Bruno. *Politics of Nature*. Cambridge, MA: Harvard University Press, 2004b.

Latour, Bruno. Politics of Nature: East and West Perspectives. *Ethics & Global Politics* 4 (2011): 71–80.

Latour, Bruno. *After Lockdown: A Metamorphosis*. Cambridge: Polity Press, 2021a.

Latour, Bruno. Is This a Dress Rehearsal? *Critical Inquiry* 47 (2021b): S25–S27.

Law, John. Culling, Catastrophe and Collectivity. *Distinktion: Scandinavian Journal of Social Theory* 9 (2008): 61–76.

Leach, Melissa, Scoones, Ian. The Social and Political Lives of Zoonotic Disease Models: Narratives, Science and Policy. *Social Science and Medicine* 88 (2013): 10–17.

Lederman, Zohar, Magalhães-Sant'Ana, Manuel, Voo, Teck Chuan. Stamping out Animal Culling: From Anthropocentrism to One Health Ethics. *Journal of Agricultural and Environmental Ethics* 34(27) (2021).

Lee, Lisa. A Bridge Back to the Future: Public Health Ethics, Bioethics, and Environmental Ethics. *American Journal of Bioethics* 17 (2017): 5–12.

Lenton, Timothy, Latour, Bruno. Gaia 2.0. *Science* 361 (2018): 1068.

Leopold, Aldo. *The Land Ethic, a Sand County Almanac: And Sketches Here and There*. Oxford: Oxford University Press, 1949.

Locke, John. *An Essay Concerning Human Understanding*. Nidditch, Peter, ed. Oxford: Clarendon Press, 1975 (original 1689).

Lohman, David, Bickford, David, Sodhi, Navjot. The Burning Issue. *Science* 316 (2007): 376.

Lowe, Philip, Whitman, Geoff, Phillipson, Jeremy. Ecology and the Social Sciences. *Journal of Applied Ecology* 46 (2009): 297–305.

Lowi, Theodore. The State of Political Science: How We Become What We Study. *American Political Science Review* 86 (1992): 1–7.

Lutz, Mark. *Economics for the Common Good: Two Centuries of Economic Thought in the Humanist Tradition*. London: Routledge, 1999.

Lynas, Mark, Houlton, Benjamin, Perry, Simon. Greater than 99% Consensus on Human Caused Climate Change in the Peer-Reviewed Scientific Literature. *Environmental Research Letters* 16 (2021): 11405.

Lysaght, Tamra, Capps, Benjamin, Bailey, Michele, et al. Justice Is the Missing Link in One Health: Results of a Mixed Methods Study in an Urban City State. *PLoS ONE* 12 (2017): e0170967.

MacGregor, Hayley, Waldman, Linda. Views from Many Worlds: Unsettling Categories in Interdisciplinary Research on Endemic Zoonotic Diseases. *Philosophical Transactions of the Royal Society B* 372 (2017): 20160170.

Macpherson, Cheryl. Global Bioethics: Did the Universal Declaration on Bioethics and Human Rights Miss the Boat? *Journal of Medical Ethics* 33 (2007): 588–90.

Majok, Aggrey, Schwabe, Calvin. *Development Among Africa's Migratory Pastoralists*. London: Bergin and Garvey, 1996.

Mann, Jonathan. Health and Human Rights: If Not Now, When? *American Journal of Public Health* 96 (1997): 1940–43.

Marí Saéz, Almudena, Weiss, Sabrina, Nowak, Kathrin, et al. Investigating the Zoonotic Origin of the West African Ebola Epidemic. *EMBO Molecular Medicine* 7 (2015): 17–23.

McCarthy, Thomas. Theory of Communicative Competence. *Philosophy of the Social Sciences* 3 (1973): 135–56.

McCloskey, Donald. Why I Am No Longer a Positivist. *Review of Social Economy* 47 (1989): 225–38.

McGraw, George. Nestle Chairman Peter Brabeck Says We Don't Have a Right to Water, Believes We Do Have a Right to Water and Everyone's Confused. *Huffington Post* 25 April (2013).

Meadows, Amanda, Stephenson, Nichole, Madhav, Nita, Oppenheim, Ben. Historical Trends Demonstrate a Pattern of Increasingly Frequent and Severe Spillover Events of High-Consequence Zoonotic Viruses. *BMJ Global Health* 8 (2023): e012026.

Medvedyuk, Stella, Govender, Piara, Raphael, Dennis. The Reemergence of Engels' Concept of Social Murder in Response to Growing Social and Health Inequalities. *Social Science & Medicine* 289 (2021): 114377.

Merton, Robert. *On the Shoulders of Giants, a Shanean Postscript, the Post-Italianate Edition*. Chicago: University of Chicago Press, 1993.

Midgley, Mary. *Beast and Man: The Roots of Human Nature*. Ithaca: Cornell University Press, 1978.

Mill, John. *Utilitarianism*. Upper Saddle River: Prentice Hall, 1957 (original 1863).

Montserrat, Agüero, Isabella, Monne, Azucena, Sánchez, et al. Highly Pathogenic Avian Influenza A(H5N1) Virus Infection in Farmed Minks, Spain, October 2022. *Eurosurveillance* 28(3) (2023): pii=2300001.

Moore, Veranus. Diseases of Animals Communicable to Man with Special Reference to those Transmitted through Milk. *The Cornell Veterinarian* 13 (1923): 292–300.

Mora, Camilo, Tittensor, Derek, Sina, Adl, Simpson, Alastair, Worm, Boris. How Many Species Are There on Earth and in the Ocean? *PLoS Biology* 9 (2011): e1001127.

Morensa, David, Daszakc, Peter, Markeld, Howard, Taubenberger, Jefferey. Pandemic COVID-19 Joins History's Pandemic Legion. *Clinical Science and Epidemiology* 11 (2020). https://doi.org/10.1128/mbio.00812–20.

Morton, Timothy. *Ecology Without Nature: Rethinking Environmental Aesthetics*. Cambridge Harvard University Press, 2007.

Mwatondo, Athman, Rahman-Shepherd, Afifah, Hollmann, Lara, et al. A Global Analysis of One Health Networks and the Proliferation of One Health Collaborations. *Lancet* 18 (2023): 605–16.

Næss, Arne. *Ecology, Community and Lifestyle: Outline of an Ecosophy*. Translated by Rothenberg David. Cambridge: Cambridge University Press, 1989 (original 1976).

Nagel, Thomas. What Is It Like to Be a Bat? *The Philosophical Review* 83 (1974): 435–50.

Nagle, John. The Idea of Pollution. *UC Davis Law Review* 43 (2009): 1–78.

Navarro, Vicente. Commentary: Is Capital the Solution or the Problem? *International Journal of Epidemiology* 33 (2004): 672–74.

Neilson, Brittany, Craig, Curtis, Altman, George, et al. Can the Biophilia Hypothesis Be Applied to Long-Duration Human Space Flight? A Mini-Review. *Frontiers in Phycology* 12 (2021): 703766.

No Author. Proceedings of Veterinary Colleges, Veterinary Medical Societies, etc. The Relation of Animals to Man. *Veterinary Journal & Annals of Comparative Pathology* 3 (1876): 457–69.

No Author. Professor Rudolf Virchow. *Popular Science Monthly* XXI (1882): 836–42.

No Author. What We Talk About When We Talk About Persons: The Language of a Legal Fiction. *Harvard Law Review* 114 (2001): 1745–68.

Nonhuman Rights Project, Inc. v Breheny (Matter of) [2022] NY Slip Op 03859 (N.Y. Ct. App. June 14, 2022).

Nussbaum, Martha. *Brief of Amicus Curiae in Support of Plaintiffs-Appellants*. APL 2021–00087; Bronx County Clerk's Index No. 260441/19; Appellate Division–First Department Case No. 2020–02581, 2020.

Nussbaum, Martha. *Justice for Animals: Our Collective Responsibility*. New York: Simon & Schuster, 2022.

Nussbaum, Martha, Nussbaum, Rachel. The Legal Status of Whales: Capabilities, Entitlements and Culture. *Revista Sequencia* 37 (2016): 19–40.

Odum, Eugene. The New Ecology. *BioScience* 14 (1964): 14–16.

Olivero, Jesús, Fa, Julia, Real, Raimundo, et al. Recent Loss of Closed Forests is Associated with Ebola Virus Disease Outbreaks. *Scientific Reports* 7 (2017): 14291.

One Health High-Level Expert Panel (OHHLEP). *One Health Theory of Change*. Geneva: World Health Organization, 2022.

O'Neill, Onora. Environmental Values, Anthropocentrism and Speciesism. *Environmental Values* 6 (1997): 127–42.

O'Neill, Onora. Kant on Duties Regarding Nonrational Nature. *Proceedings of the Aristotelian Society, Supplementary Volumes* 72 (1998): 211–28.

O'Neill, Onora. *Bounds of Justice*. Cambridge: Cambridge University Press, 2000.

Osler, William. *Science and Immortality*. Cambridge: The Riverside Press, 1904.

Osofsky, Steve, Karesh, William, Kock, Richard, Kock, Michael. *AHEAD Invitees' Briefing Packet. Southern and East African Experts Panel on Designing Successful Conservation and Development Interventions at the Wildlife/Livestock Interface: Implications for Wildlife, Livestock, and Human Health. Animal Health for the Environment and Development*. IUCN Vth World Parks Congress 14–15 September, Durban, 2003.

Osofsky, Steven, Kock, Richard, Kock, Michael, et al. Building Support for Protected Areas Using a 'One Health' Perspective. In McNeely, Jeffrey, ed. *Friends for Life: New Partners in Support of Protected Areas*. Gland: World Conservation Union, 2005: 65–79.

Ostfeld, Richard. *Lyme Disease: The Ecology of a Complex System*. Oxford: Oxford University Press, 2011.

Ostrom, Elanor. Polycentric Systems for Coping with Collective Action and Global Environmental Change. *Global Environmental Change* 20 (2010): 550–57.

Ostrom, Elinor. A Diagnostic Approach for Going beyond Panaceas. *Proceedings of the National Academies of Science* 104 (2007): 15181–87.

Paget, Stephen. *For and Against Experiments on Animals: Evidence Before the Royal Commission on Vivisection*. London: H. K. Lewis, 1902.

Perry, John, Perry, Jane. *Veterinarians and What They Do*. New York: F. Watts, 1914.

Pintér, László, Offerdahl, Kate, Almassy, Dora, Offerdahl, Kate, Czunyi, Sarah. *Global Goals and the Environment: Progress and Prospects*. Winnipeg: International Institute for Sustainable Development, 2015.

Pluhar, Evelyn. Moral Agents and Moral Patients. *Between the Species* 4 (1988): 32–45.

Porter, Roy. *Enlightenment: Britain and the Creation of the Modern World.* London: Allen Lane, 2000.

Porter, Roy. *Flesh in the Age of Reason.* London: Allen Lane, 2003.

Potter, Van Resseler. *Global Bioethics: Building on the Leopold Legacy.* East Lansing: Michigan University Press, 1988.

Quammen, David. *Spillover: Animal Infections and the Next Human Pandemic.* New York: W.W. Norton, 2012.

Rawls, John. *A Theory of Justice.* Cambridge Harvard University Press, 1971.

Regan, Tom. *The Case for Animal Rights.* Berkeley: University of California Press, 1983.

Rodriguez, Mario-Henry. Foreword. In Charron, Dominique, ed. *Ecohealth Research in Practice: Innovative Applications of an Ecosystem Approach to Health.* Ottawa: Springer, 2012: v–viii.

Rolston III, Holmes. Is There an Ecological Ethic? *Ethics* 85 (1975): 93–109.

Rome, Adam. Give Earth a Chance: The Environmental Movement and the Sixties. *Journal of American History* 90 (2003): 525–54.

Routley, Richard. Is There a Need for a New, an Environmental, Ethic? *Proceedings of the XVth World Congress of Philosophy* 1 (1973): 205–10.

Rush, Benjamin. Lecture III. *Medical Inquiries and Observations.* Volume 1. 3rd ed. District of Pennsylvania: Hopkins and Earle; Mathew Carey Johnson, and Warner; Kimber and Conrad; Bradford and Inskeep, Thomas and William Bradford; Benjamin and Thomas Kite; and Bennett and Walton, 1809.

Rush, Benjamin. On the Duty and Advantages of Studying the Diseases of Domestic Animals, and the Remedies Proper to Remove Them. In Rush, Benjamin, ed. *Sixteen Introductory Lectures, to Courses of Lectures upon the Institutes and Practice of Medicine.* Philadelphia: Bradford and Innskeep, 1811: 295–317.

Rutz, Christian, Loretto, Matthias-Claudio, Bates, et al. COVID-19 Lockdowns Allow Researchers to Quantify the Effects of Human Activity on Wildlife. *Nature Ecology & Evolution* 4 (2020): 1156–59.

Ryan, Sadie, Walsh, Peter. Consequences of Non-Intervention for Infectious Disease in African Great Apes. *PLoS One* 6 (2011): e29030.

Sachs, Jeffrey, Kroll, Christian, Lafortune, Guillame, Fuller, Grayson, Woelm, Finn. *Sustainable Development Report 2021.* Cambridge: Cambridge University Press, 2021.

Sanders, Clinton, Arluke, Arnold. If Lions Could Speak: Investigating the Animal-Human Relationship and the Perspectives of Nonhuman Others. *The Sociological Quarterly* 34 (1993): 377–90.

Sanderson, Steven. The Future of Conservation. *Foreign Affairs* 81 (2002): 162–73.

Sass, Hans-Martin. Fritz Jahr's 1927 Concept of Bioethics. *Kennedy Institute of Ethics Journal* 17 (2007): 279–95.

Saunders, L. Z. Virchow's Contributions to Veterinary Medicine: Celebrated Then, Forgotten Now. *Veterinary Pathology* 37 (2000): 199–207.

Schmidt, Carl. Editorial: One Medicine for More than One World. *Circulation Research* 11 (1962): 901–3.

Schwabe, Calvin. *Cattle, Priests, and Progress in Medicine* (Volume 4). Minneapolis: University of Minnesota, 1978.

Schwabe, Calvin. *Veterinary Medicine and Human Health*. 3rd ed. Baltimore: Williams & Wilkins, 1984.

Schwabe, Calvin. History of the Scientific Relationships of Veterinary Public Health. *Revue Scientifique et Technique* 10 (1991): 933–49.

Schwabe, Calvin. The Current Epidemiological Revolution in Veterinary Medicine. Part II. *Preventive Veterinary Medicine* 18 (1993): 3–16.

Schwabe, Calvin. Integrated Delivery of Primary Health Care for Humans and Animals. *Agriculture and Human Values* 15 (1998): 121–25.

Searle, Adam, Turnbull, Jonathon. Resurgent Natures? More-Than-Human Perspectives on COVID-19. *Dialogues in Human Geography* 10 (2020): 291–95.

Selter, Felicitas, Salloch, Sabine. Whose Health and Which Health? Two Theoretical Flaws in the One Health Paradigm. *Bioethics* 37 (2023): 674–82.

Sen, Amartya. *Human Rights and Asian Values*. 16th Morganthau Memorial Lecture on Ethics and Foreign Policy. New York: Carnegie Council on Ethics and International Affairs, 1997.

Sims, Les, Ellis, Trevor, Liu, Kaituo, et al. Avian Influenza in Hong Kong 1997–2002. *Avian Diseases* 47(s3) (2003): 832–38.

Smil, Vaclav. *The Earth's Biosphere: Evolution, Dynamics, and Change*. Cambridge MIT Press, 2002.

Smith, Maxwell, Thompson, Alison, Upshur, Ross. Is 'Health Equity' Bad for Our Health? A Qualitative Empirical Ethics Study of Public Health Policy-Makers' Perspectives. *Canadian Journal of Public Health* 109 (2018): 633–42.

Spaiser, Viktoria, Ranganathan, Shyam, Bali Swain, Ranjula, Sumpter, David. The Sustainable Development Oxymoron: Quantifying and Modelling the Incompatibility of Sustainable Development Goals. *International Journal of Sustainable Development & World Ecology* 24 (2017): 457–70.

Spencer, Julia, McRobie, Ellen, Dar, Osman, et al. Is the Current Surge in Political and Financial Attention to One Health Solidifying or Splintering the Movement? *BMJ Global Health* 4 (2019): e001102.

Steffen, Will, Crutzen, Paul, McNeill, John. The Anthropocene: Are Humans Now Overwhelming the Great Forces of Nature? *Ambio* 8 (2007): 614–21.

Steger, Florian. Fritz Jahr's (1895–1953) European Concept of Bioethics and Its Application Potential. *JAHR* 6/2 (2015): 215–22.

Stone, Christopher. Should Trees Have Standing – Toward Legal Rights for Natural Objects. *Southern California Law Review* 45 (1972): 450–501.

Stop Ecocide Foundation. *Independent Expert Panel for the Legal Definition of Ecocide: Commentary and Core Text.* June (2021): www.stopecocide.earth/ legal-definition.

Suddendorf, Thomas. *The Gap: The Science of What Separates Us from Other Animals.* New York: Basic Books, 2013.

Szasz, Kathleen. *Petishism: Pets and Their People in the Western World.* New York: Holt, Rinehart and Winston, 1969.

Tansley, Arthur. *Practical Plant Ecology.* London: George Allen & Unwin, 1923.

Tarlock, Dan. Is There a There There in Environmental Law? *Journal of Land Use and Environmental Law* 19 (2004): 213–54.

Taylor, Paul. *Respect for Nature: A Theory of Environmental Ethics.* Princeton: Princeton University Press, 1986.

Taylor, Thomas. *A Vindication of the Rights of Brutes* (original 1792). A Facsimile Reproduction with an Introduction by Louise Schutz Boas. Gainesville: Scholars' Facsimiles & Reprints, 1966.

Teilhard de Chardin, Pierre. *Man's Place in Nature.* New York: Harper & Row, 1966.

Langton, Thomas, Jones, Mark, McGill, Iain. Analysis of the Impact of Badger Culling on Bovine Tuberculosis in Cattle in the High-Risk Area of England, 2009–2020. *Veterinary Record* 190 (2022): e1384.

Toddington, Stuart. Agency, Authority and the Logic of Mutual Recognition. *Ratio Juris* 28 (2013): 89–109.

Unknown Author. A Review of the Doctrine of Disease, Taught at Present by Benjamin Rush, M. D. Professor of the Institute and Practice of Medicine, Etc. in the University of Pennsylvania. In Hosack, David, and Wakefield Francis, John, eds. *The American Medical and Philosophical Register*, Volume 1. New York: C. S. Van Winkle, 1811: 49–60 (Part I) & 160–168 (Part II).

United Nations' High-Level Expert Group on the Net Zero Emissions Commitments of Non-State Entities. *Integrity Matters: Net Zero Commitments by Businesses, Financial Institutions, Cities and Regions.* March 2022.

United Nations Environment Programme (UNEP). *For People and Planet: The United Nations Environment Programme Strategy for 2022–2025 to Tackle*

Climate Change, Loss of Nature and Pollution. UNEP/EA.5/3/Rev.1. 17 February 2021.

United Nations (UN). *Promotion and Protection of All Human Rights, Civil, Political, Economic, Social and Cultural Rights, Including the Right to Development.* A/HRC/RES/48/13, 18 October 2021.

United Nations (UN). *Ecosystem Approach.* COP 5 Decision V/6. Fifth Ordinary Meeting of the Conference of the Parties to the Convention on Biological Diversity, 15–26 May 2000.

United Nations (UN). *Harmony with Nature: Report of the Secretary-General.* A/74/236, 2019.

United Nations (UN). *The Millennium Development Goals Report 2015.* New York: United Nations, 2015.

United Nations (UN). *The Human Right to Water and Sanitation.* A/RES/64/292, 3 August 2010.

Vernadsky, Vladimir. *The Biosphere.* New York: Springer-Verlag, 1998 (original 1926).

Verweij, Marcel, Bovenkerk, Bernice. Ethical Promises and Pitfalls of OneHealth. *Public Health Ethics* 9 (2016): 1–4.

Virchow, Rudolf. An Address on the Value of Pathological Experiments. *British Medical Journal* 2 (1881): 198–203.

Waldron, Jeremy. Judges as Moral Reasoners. *International Journal of Constitutional Law* 7 (2009): 2–24.

Wallace, Robert, Bergmann, Luke, Kock, Richard, et al. The Dawn of Structural One Health: A New Science Tracking Disease Emergence Along Circuits of Capital. *Social Science & Medicine* 129 (2015) 68–77.

Warner, Bernhard. Invasion of the 'Frankenbees': The Danger of Building a Better Bee. *Guardian* 16 October (2018).

Warren, Mary Anne. The Rights of the Nonhuman World. In Elliot, Robert and Gare, Arran, eds. *Environmental Philosophy: A Collection of Readings.* University Park: The Pennsylvania State University Press, 1983: 109–34.

Weiss, Rick. Africa's Apes Are Imperilled, Researchers Warn. *The Washington Post* 7 April (2003): A.07.

Whitehead, Hal, Rendell, Luke. *The Cultural Lives of Whales and Dolphins.* Chicago: University of Chicago Press, 2015.

Whitmee, Sarah, Haines, Andy, Beyrer, Chris, et al. Safeguarding Human Health in the Anthropocene Epoch: Report of the Rockefeller Foundation–Lancet Commission on Planetary Health. *Lancet* 386 (2015): 1973–2028.

Williams, Bernard. The Human Prejudice. In Moore, A. ed., *Philosophy as a Humanistic Discipline.* Princeton: Princeton University Press, 2006: 135–52.

Wilson, Edward. *Sociobiology: The New Synthesis*. Cambridge: The Belknap Press of Harvard University Press, 1975.

Wise, Steven. *Rattling the Cage: Toward Legal Rights for Animals*. Cambridge: Perseus Books, 2000.

Wolfe, Nathan, Escalante, Ananias, Karesh, William, et al. Wild Primate Populations in Emerging Infectious Disease Research: The Missing Link? *Emerging Infectious Diseases* 4 (1998): 149–58.

Wolfrum, Rüdiger, Matz, Nele. The Interplay of the United Nations Convention on the Law of the Sea and the Convention on Biological Diversity. *Max Planck Yearbook of United Nations Law* 4 (2000): 445–80.

Woods, Abigail, Bresalier, Michael, Cassidy, Angela, Dentinger, Rachel. Introduction: Centering Animals Within Medical History. In Woods, Abigail, Bresalier, Michael, Cassidy, Angela, and Dentinger, Rachel, eds. *Animals and the Shaping of Modern Medicine: One Health and Its Histories*. Cham: Palgrave Macmillan, 2018: 1–26.

World Bank. *Putting Pandemics Behind Us: Investing in One Health to Reduce Risks of Emerging Infectious Diseases*. Washington, DC: International Bank for Reconstruction and Development/The World Bank, 2022.

World Health Organisation (WHO). *Joint Tripartite (FAO, OIE, WHO) and UNEP Statement*. 1 December 2021.

World Health Organisation (WHO). COVID-19 – Denmark. *Disease Outbreak News* 3 December (2020).

World Health Organisation (WHO). *Ethical Considerations for Use of Unregistered Interventions for Ebola Viral Disease. Report of an Advisory Panel to the WHO*. WHO/HIS/KER/GHE/14.1. 2014b.

World Health Organisation (WHO). *Statement on the 1st Meeting of the IHR Emergency Committee on the 2014 Ebola Outbreak in West Africa*. 8 August 2014a.

World Organisation for Animal Health. *Terrestrial Code*. 3rd ed. OIE – Terrestrial Animal Health Code, 2022: www.woah.org/en/what-we-do/stand ards/codes-and-manuals/terrestrial-code-online-access/.

Zinsstag, Jakob, Kaiser-Grolimund, Andrea, Heitz-Tokpa, Kathrin, et al. Advancing One Human–Animal–Environment Health for Global Health Security: What Does the Evidence Say? *Lancet* 401 (2023): 591–604.

Zinsstag, Jakob, Schelling, Esther, Wyss, Kaspar, Mahamat, Mahamat Bechir. Potential of Cooperation between Human and Animal Health to Strengthen Health Systems. *Lancet* 366 (2005): 2142–5.

Zwarthoed, Danielle. Should Future Generations Be Content with Plastic Trees and Singing Electronic Birds? *Journal of Agricultural and Environmental Ethics* 29 (2016): 219–36.

Cambridge Elements ☰

Bioethics and Neuroethics

Thomasine Kushner

California Pacific Medical Center, San Francisco

Thomasine Kushner, PhD, is the founding Editor of the *Cambridge Quarterly of Healthcare Ethics* and coordinates the International Bioethics Retreat, where bioethicists share their current research projects, the Cambridge Consortium for Bioethics Education, a growing network of global bioethics educators, and the Cambridge-ICM Neuroethics Network, which provides a setting for leading brain scientists and ethicists to learn from each other.

About the Series

Bioethics and neuroethics play pivotal roles in today's debates in philosophy, science, law, and health policy. With the rapid growth of scientific and technological advances, their importance will only increase. This series provides focused and comprehensive coverage in both disciplines consisting of foundational topics, current subjects under discussion and views toward future developments.

Cambridge Elements ≡

Bioethics and Neuroethics

Printed in the United States
by Baker & Taylor Publisher Services